Grammar
in practice 3

40 units of
self-study
grammar
exercises

Roger Gower

with tests

CAMBRIDGE
UNIVERSITY PRESS

PUBLISHED BY THE PRESS SYNDICATE OF THE UNIVERSITY OF CAMBRIDGE
The Pitt Building, Trumpington Street, Cambridge, United Kingdom

CAMBRIDGE UNIVERSITY PRESS
The Edinburgh Building, Cambridge CB2 2RU, UK
40 West 20th Street, New York, NY 10011–4211, USA
477 Williamstown Road, Port Melbourne, VIC 3207, Australia
Ruiz de Alarcón 13, 28014 Madrid, Spain
Dock House, The Waterfront, Cape Town 8001, South Africa

http://www.cambridge.org

First published 2004

Produced by Kamae Design, Oxford.

Printed in Italy by G. Canale & C. S.p.A.

Typeface Bembo 10.5/12pt. *System* QuarkXpress® [KAMAE]

A catalogue record for this book is available from the British Library

ISBN 0 521 54041 0 paperback

Contents

1 Is it a good job?

be/have got

Questions				Short answers				
Am	I			I	**am**.		I'm not.	
Is	he/she/it	late?	Yes,	he/she/it	**is**.	No,	he/she/it	**isn't** ('s not).
Are	we/you/they			we/you/they	**are**.		we/you/they	**aren't** ('re not).
Have	I/you/we/they	got a pool?	Yes,	I/you/we/they	**have**.	No,	I/you/we/they	**haven't**.
Has	he/she/it			he/she/it	**has**.		he/she/it	**hasn't**.

A Write questions with *be* and *have got* for a questionnaire.

LIFE AT WORK

❶ you/interesting job? *Have you got an interesting job?*
❷ your job/difficult?
❸ you/happy at work?
❹ you/a lot of friends at work?
❺ your colleagues/helpful?
❻ your manager/pleased with your work?
❼ you/a company car?
❽ your company/a gym?

B Answer the questions about you and your life at work.

1 *Yes, I have./No, I haven't.*
2
3
4
5
6
7
8

2 We had a big house

	have	have got
Present	I **have** a headache but I **don't have** any aspirins. **Do** you **have** a headache? Yes, I **do**. / No, I **don't**.	I'**ve got** a headache but I **haven't got** any aspirins. **Have** you **got** a headache? Yes, I **have**. / No, I **haven't**.
Past	I **had** a headache last night but I **didn't have** any aspirins. **Did** you **have** a headache last night? Yes, I **did**. No, I **didn't**.	ⓘ We don't usually use **have got** for the past.

We also use have to talk about an action in some expressions: *have a wash, have a swim, have a meeting, have a meal, have good weather*
ⓘ We can't use **have got** with these expressions.

A Complete the sentences with the correct form of *have* or *have got*.

HONG KONG FACTFILE

1 Hong Kong *has got* 23 parks and 40% of it is green!

2 In 1840, Hong Kong *had* a population of only 6,000.

3 Hong Kong *doesn't have* many rivers, so most of its water comes from China.

4 Hong Kong *has got* seven large yacht clubs.

6 It *has* hot summers and cool, dry winters.

5 Many visitors come to Hong Kong and *have* a fantastic meal in one of its 6,000 restaurants!

B Use *have/have got* to make sentences about your town.

Today:

1 My town *'s got / has/hasn't got / doesn't have a lot of parks.* (a lot of parks)

2 It *has a lot of expensive shops* (a lot of expensive shops)

3 We ....

In 1900:

4 It *didn't have a big population* (a big population)

5 My town ....

6 We ....

3 People are living longer

Present continuous

Positive			Negative		
I'm			I'm not (am not)		
He/She/It's (is)		singing.	He/She/It	isn't (is not)	eating.
We/You/They're (are)			You/we/they	aren't (are not)	

Questions			Short answers					
Am	I			I	am.		I'm not.	
Is	he/she/it	working?	Yes,	he/she/it	is.	No,	he/she/it	isn't.
Are	we/you/they			we/you/they	are		we/you/they	aren't.

My French is getting better. (The situation is changing.)

A Complete the sentences with the correct form of the verbs.

hold ✓   ~~look~~   smile   stand ✓   talk   wear ✓

1 A mother _____is looking_____ out of an open door.

2 Perhaps she _____ to someone.

3 Another woman and a child _____ behind the wall.

4 The woman _____ the child's hand.

5 They _____ long dresses and hats.

6 The woman _____ but the child is.

Courtyard in Delft Hooch

B Write the questions in the present continuous.

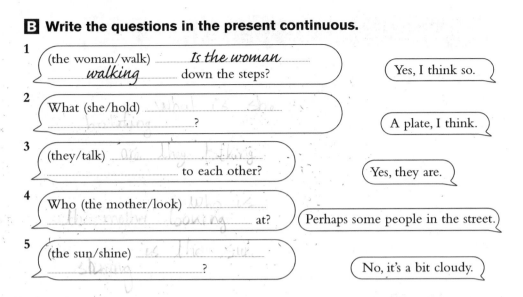

1 (the woman/walk) _Is the woman walking_ down the steps?

Yes, I think so.

2 What (she/hold) _____ ?

A plate, I think.

3 (they/talk) _____ to each other?

Yes, they are.

4 Who (the mother/look) _____ at?

Perhaps some people in the street.

5 (the sun/shine) _____ ?

No, it's a bit cloudy.

C How is life changing in the UK? Complete the sentences in the correct form of the present continuous.

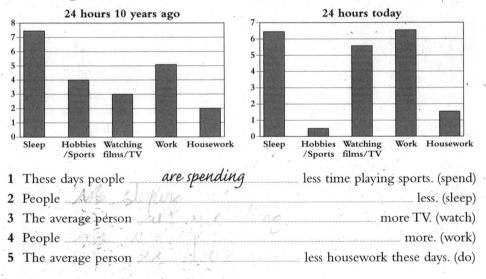

1 These days people _are spending_ less time playing sports. (spend)
2 People _____ less. (sleep)
3 The average person _____ more TV. (watch)
4 People _____ more. (work)
5 The average person _____ less housework these days. (do)

D How is life changing in your country?

1 (watch more TV/watch less TV) Children _are watching more/less TV._
2 (work more/work less) Old people _____
3 (stay single/get married) More people _____
4 (get bigger/get smaller) Families _____
5 (leave home earlier/leave home later) Children _____

7

4 They speak Spanish

Present simple

Positive		Negative	
I/You/We/They	**work**.	I/You/We/They	**don't (do not) work**.
He/She/It	**works**.	He/She/It	**doesn't (does not) work**.

Questions			Answers					
Do	I/you/ we/they	**work**?	Yes,	I/you/ we/they	**do**.	No,	I/you/ we/they	**don't**.
Does	he/she/it			he/she/it	**does**.		he/she/it	**doesn't**.

A Complete the tourist guide. Use the verbs in the present simple.

~~be~~ eat have play ~~speak~~ wear not/understand

There (1) _____*are*_____ two official languages in Peru, Spanish and Quechua (the language of the Incas). Peru also (2) __*have*_____ many other native languages and today some people still (3) __*speak*_____ Spanish. Luckily for British tourists, Peruvians in tourist areas often (4) _____ English. The Andes mountains is the area of Quechua and many people still (5) _____ traditional music and (6) _____ traditional clothes. Visitors love Peruvian food and (7) _____ a lot of ceviche (raw fish in lemon juice).

B Write the verbs in the correct form of the present simple. Then match the questions with the answers below.

Where in the World?

1 Where (people/read) __*do people read*__ more books per person than anywhere else? ___*C*___

2 Where (the world's fastest land animals/live) _____ ? _____

3 Where (90% of families/own) _____ video-recorders – the highest number in the world?

4 Where (the New Year/last) _____ three days and (take place) _____ at the beginning of February?

5 Where (restaurants/serve) _____ no beef – only chicken, lamb and fish?

6 Where (people/eat) _____ more cheese than anywhere else in the world?

A Australia   B Africa   C Iceland   D India   E France   F China

C Write sentences about these people. Use the verbs in brackets.

THE WORLD'S RICH LIST

Name		Money comes from	Interests
Bill Gates	USA	Computer software	Books and golf
Nina Wang	Hong Kong	Property	Comic books
Bernie and Slavica Ecclestone	Britain	Motor racing	Politics
Rob Walton	USA	Supermarkets	Old cars
Kenneth Thomson and family	Canada	Newspapers	Art
Sheikh Makhtoum	Dubai	Oil	Horseracing

1 Bill Gates _designs software and plays golf._ (design/play)
2 Nina Wang _____ (sell/write)
3 Bernie and Slavica Ecclestone _____ (live in/be interested in)
4 Rob Walton _____ (own/drive)
5 Kenneth Thomson and family _____ (sell/collect)
6 Sheikh Makhtoum _____ (come from/like)

D Correct the information in these newspapers.

1   Bill hates reading.

No, he _doesn't. He likes reading._

2   Nina lives in Japan.

No, she _____

3   The Ecclestones make their money from newspapers.

No, they _____

4   Rob comes from Germany.

No, he _____

5   The Thomsons hate art.

No, they _____

6   Sheikh Makhtoum works in the property business.

No, he _____

5 She's never ill

A Write sentences about Karen.

Name: Karen Jennings

How often do you ...
get a cold? Not often.
go to the doctor? About three
times a year.
have a headache? Sometimes in
the evenings.
feel depressed? Rarely.
stay off work? Hardly ever!
get some exercise? Every day.

1 *She doesn't often get a cold.*

2 _____

3 _____

4 _____

5 _____

6 _____

B How often do you do the things below? Write sentences.

1 play golf *I never play golf.*
2 go jogging _____
3 go swimming _____
4 play football _____
5 go for a walk _____
6 play tennis _____

6 I'm travelling round the world

Present simple or present continuous?

We use the present simple:
for something which is always true (a fact): The sun **rises** in the east.
for something we often/usually do: He **watches** television every evening.
with verbs which describe a state not an action (*like, love, hate, understand, believe, want, know, think*): He **understands** Spanish. I **like** you. NOT ~~I am liking you.~~

We use the present continuous:
for something which is happening at the moment of speaking: Where's Jenny? She**'s watching** television.
for temporary situations: I**'m learning** English at college.
for changing situations: My French **is getting** better.

ⓘ I **live** in France. (It's my home.)
I**'m living** in France. (Now, but it's temporary.)

A This is an article about the movie star, Susan Sarandon. Underline the correct form.

Susan Sarandon **(1) is usually living/usually lives** in New York with the actor, Tim Robbins. At the moment **(2) she's working/works** for UNICEF in India, meeting sick children. **(3)** She **'s liking/likes** trips like this but there is a lot to do and **(4) she's never getting/never gets** much sleep. Tim **(5) isn't travelling/doesn't travel** with Susan when she works for UNICEF. **(6)** He's **making/makes** a film in Hollywood at the moment.

B Write the journalist's questions and Susan's answers using the article in A.

1 *Do you usually live in New York?*   *Yes, I do.*
2 Where do you work?
3 Do you like trips?
4 Does Tim travel with Susan when she works for UNITE?
5
6 What He is doing in Hollywood?

C Complete the sentences about Irek Mukhamedov. Use verbs from the box in the correct form of the present simple or continuous.

> act ~~dance~~ not/dance like live watch

CELEBRITY PROFILE

NAME
Irek Mukhamedov

OCCUPATION
Ballet dancer with the Royal Ballet

FAMILY
Wife Masha and son and daughter

WORK AT PRESENT
Actor in TV hospital drama

LIKES
Dancing, acting

1 Normally Irek __dances__ with the Royal Ballet.

2 This week he _is acting_ in a TV hospital drama.

3 He _likes_ acting very much.

4 At the moment he _is dancing_ with the Royal Ballet.

5 He _lives_ with his wife, Masha, and his son and daughter.

6 Right now his children _are watching_ their dad on TV!

D Write the questions in the present simple or continuous.

1 (you/like/ballet) _Do you like ballet?_

2 (you/watch TV/at the moment) _are you watching Tv ?_

3 (you/sometimes/listen to music at work) _Do you listen to music at work?_

4 (your family/live/with you) _Do you live with you family?_

5 (where/you/do this exercise) _Where are you doing this exercice ?_

6 (what/you/want to do later today) _What Do you want to do later too?_

E Answer the questions in D for you.

1 _Yes, I do./No, I don't._   4

2   5

3   6

7 She studied business

Past simple (regular and irregular verbs) ▸▸ Irregular forms page 61

	Positive	Questions		
I/He/She/It We/You/They	**stayed** last night. **left** yesterday.	**Did**	I/he/she/it we/you/they	**stay** last night? **leave** yesterday?
	Negative	Short answers		
	didn't stay last night.	Yes,	I/he/she/it/	**did**.
	didn't leave yesterday.	No,	we/you/they	**didn't**.

Verb *be*

Positive and negative			Questions		
I/He/She/It	**was/wasn't**	at home.	**Was**	I/he/she/it	at home?
We/You/They	**were/weren't**		**Were**	we/you/they	

Short answers					
Yes,	I/he/she/it	**was**.	No,	I/he/she/it	**wasn't**
	we/you/they	**were**		we/you/they	**weren't**.

A | Complete the sentences below with the past simple.

Key events in Business History

1	1499-1000 BC	The Phoenicians _opened_ (open) sea ports in the Mediterranean.
2	687 BC	The Lydians _used_ (use) coins as money for the first time.
3	599-500 BC	The Babylonians _sat up_ (set up) the first banks.
4	1260	Florence _became_ (become) the centre of world banking.
5	1859	The USA _sold_ (sell) oil for the first time.
6	1958	The Bank of America _introduced_ (introduce) the world's first credit card.
7	1999	Europe _started_ (start) a new currency, the Euro.

B | Complete this company report. Write the verbs in the past simple.

Last year we **(1 have)** _had_ another excellent year at The Motor Company.
We **(2 open)** _opened_ a new factory in the north of the country and we
(3 make) _made_ 10% more cars. This **(4 create)** _created_ over 500 new
jobs. Sales **(5 be)** _were_ very good in the UK but unfortunately, because the price of
oil **(6 go)** _went_ up at the beginning of the year, we **(7 not/sell)** _didn't sell_
as many cars in Europe and the USA as we hoped. However, we **(8 do)** _did_ better
than all the other big car companies. Finally, we **(9 win)** _won_ the prize for best
small car of the year.

C Complete the questions in this questionnaire in the past simple.

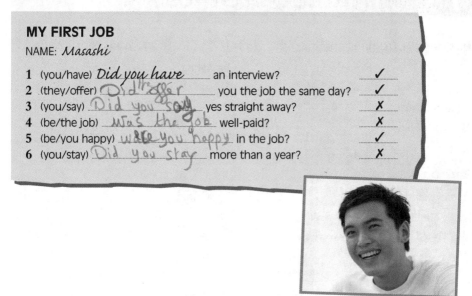

MY FIRST JOB

NAME: *Masashi*

1 (you/have) *Did you have* .... an interview? ✓
2 (they/offer) *Did offer* .... you the job the same day? ✓
3 (you/say) *Did you say* .... yes straight away? ✗
4 (be/the job) *Was the job* .... well-paid? ✗
5 (be/you happy) *Were you happy* .... in the job? ✓
6 (you/stay) *Did you stay* .... more than a year? ✗

D Write short answers for Masashi, then for you.

Masashi

1 *Yes, he did.*
2
3
4
5
6

You

1 *Yes, I did. /No, I didn't.*
2
3
4
5
6

E Write sentences to say what you did or didn't do at work yesterday. Use the following verbs.

arrive (late)   get (more than 10 emails)   use (a photocopier)   write (a report)
have (a long lunch)   shout (at the manager)   go (to sleep)   make (a mistake)
enjoy (work)   leave (early)

1 *I didn't arrive late. I wrote a report.*
2
3
4
5
6

8 Who phoned you?

Object and subject questions

Object					Object	
Who		**are**	you	asking to the party?	**John.**	I'm asking **John.**
What		**did**	he	bring?	**Nothing.**	He brought **nothing.**
Which	bus	**do**	you	take to work?	**The 74.**	I take **the 74.**
How many	people	**does**	she	know?	**A lot.**	She knows **a lot.**
Subject					Subject	
Who		came to the party?			**John.**	**John** did./**John** came.
What		is happening?			**Nothing.**	**Nothing**'s happening.
Which bus		leaves first?			**The 18.**	**The 18** does.
How many (people)		work here?			**50.**	**50** people work here.

A Complete the questions and underline the correct answer.

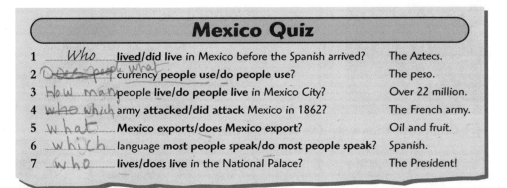

Mexico Quiz

1 _Who_ <u>lived</u>/did live in Mexico before the Spanish arrived?   The Aztecs.
2 ~~Does people~~ What currency people use/<u>do people use</u>?   The peso.
3 _How many_ people live/<u>do people live</u> in Mexico City?   Over 22 million.
4 ~~who~~ which army attacked/<u>did attack</u> Mexico in 1862?   The French army.
5 _what_ Mexico exports/<u>does Mexico export</u>?   Oil and fruit.
6 _which_ language <u>most people speak</u>/do most people speak?   Spanish.
7 _who_ <u>lives</u>/does live in the National Palace?   The President!

B Complete the questions using the verb in brackets in the past.

FOREIGN TRAVEL QUESTIONNAIRE (BUSINESS TRIP TO ACAPULCO)

1 (airline/use) _Which airline did you use?_ Mexicana
2 (people/travel) _How many people travelled_ with you? Two.
3 (pay) _Who payed_ for your trip? The company.
4 (meet/you) _who met you_ at the airport? Nobody. We took a taxi.
5 (hotel/stay at) ~~where~~ which hotel stayed at? The Royal.
6 (other companies/visit) _How many_ ? Three.
7 (pay) _How payed_ the hotel bill? Our Mexican partners.

9 They were reading

Past continuous

Positive				Negative		
I/He/She	**was**	reading		I/He/She	**wasn't (was not)**	reading.
You/We/They	**were**			You/We/They	**weren't (were not)**	

Questions								
Was	I/he/she/it	working?	Yes,	I/he/she/it	**was**.	No,	I/he/she/it	**wasn't**.
Were	we/you/they			we/you/they	**were**.		we/you/they	**weren't**.

A Complete the story with verbs from the box. Use the past continuous.

> dance   not/enjoy   hit   ~~learn~~   teach   wish

Billy (1) _____was learning_____ to box in the school gym.
He (2) _____was_____ the punchbag but he
(3) _____ it. Next door Mrs Wilkinson
(4) _____ the ballet class. The girls
(5) _____ . Billy watched the ballet dancers.
He (6) _____ that he could dance too.

B Complete these stories with the past continuous.

Monika (1) _____was watching_____ (watch) the flying show in Stockholm.
Planes (2) ___were flying___ (fly) high above in the clouds. A young man
(3) ___was standing___ (stand) next to her. He (4) ___was wearing___
(wear) red, white and blue shorts and he (5) ___was holding___ (hold) a
glass of beer in his hand. He (6) ___was singing___ (sing) very loudly. The
football fan pulled her towards him. 'Give me a kiss', he said. The other people
(7) ___weren't looking___ (not look) at them. They (8) ___were watching___
(watch) the show. She quickly hit him hard in the stomach.

DOUBLE CROSS
PHILIP PROWSE

Charlie and Susie (9) ___were walking___ (walk) in the country.
The sun (10) ___was shining___ (shine) and the birds
(11) ___were singing___ (sing). It was a beautiful autumn day.
Suddenly, they stopped. Some sheep (12) ___were running___ (run)
across one of the fields. Something (13) ___was running___ (run)
after them!

Adapted from CUP readers *Double Cross* by Philip Prowse and *The Beast* by Carolyn Walker.

10 It was raining. Did you go out?

Past continuous or past simple?

We use the past simple for:
finished actions. We **walked** to the station. (We finished our journey.)
verbs describing states. (*like, love, hate, understand, believe, want, know, think*): I **didn't**
understand her. NOT ~~I wasn't understanding her~~.

We use the past continuous for:
unfinished actions. At 8.30 we **were walking** to the station. (We were in the middle
of our journey.)
general description. The sun **was shining**.
a long action which is interrupted by a shorter action: They **were having** lunch (a long
action) when the phone **rang** (a short action in the middle).

A Read the magazine article and write the journalist's questions.

HOLIDAY DISASTERS

Luke and Amy (1) were looking forward to their holiday. Unfortunately, when they arrived
at their destination (2) it was raining hard. They got into a taxi and were driving into the
city centre when suddenly (3) a wheel came off. They (4) decided to walk the rest of the
way and were checking into their hotel (5) when Amy realised they had the wrong
suitcases. Then, when (6) Luke was telephoning the airport, all the lights went out. What a
way to start a holiday!

1 Were *you looking forward to your holiday* ?
2 Was *it raining* ?
3 When did the *wheel came off* ?
4 What did ?
5 When *Amy did realised* you had the wrong suitcases?
6 What *Luke did* when all the lights went out?

B Now write Luke and Amy's answers.

1 *Yes, we were.*
2
3 When we
4
5 When we
6 I

C On this website people talk about their dreams. Write the verbs in the past simple or continuous.

Dream talk

My dream.

1 We (watch) *were watching* TV when a strange man (break) *broke* into our house.

2 I (sing) *was singing* in a concert when I (lose) *lost* my voice.

3 We (drop) *dropped* our favourite mirror as we (carry) *were carrying* it along a street.

4 I (see) *saw* Elvis. He (sit) *was sitting* on a train.

5 The police (stop) *stopped* me because I (not/wear) *wasn't / wearing* any clothes.

6 My wife and I (lie) *were lying* on a beach. We (not/know) *didn't / know* where we were.

7 A lot of people (run) *running* after me when suddenly I (start) *started* to fly.

D Write the questions people asked about the dreams in Exercise C.

1 (he/have) *Did he have* a gun?

2 (you/sing) *Did was you Singing* in front of a lot of people?

3 (Where/you/take) *Where you were taking* the mirror at the time?

4 (he/see) *Did you see he* you?

5 (What/they/say) ____ to you?

6 (other people/lie) ____ on the beach?

7 (Why/they/run) ____ after you?

E Answer these questions for you about last night.

1 What were you doing at 8 o'clock last night? *I was reading a book.*

2 What were you doing at 10 o'clock? ____

3 What was the last thing you did before you went to sleep? ____

4 Were people watching TV in your house/flat when you went to sleep? ____

5 Did you have a dream last night? ____

6 Were you in the dream? ____

7 How did you feel when you woke up? ____

Test 1 (Units 1–10)

A Circle the correct form.

1 Have you **a new manager got**/**got a new manager**?
2 We **had**/**had got** a long meeting yesterday.
3 Why the **man is**/**is the man** looking at you?
4 I'm **believing**/**believe** you.
5 She **takes never**/**never takes** a holiday.
6 At the moment **I'm writing**/**write** an email.
7 Did you **get**/**got** up early?
8 Who **does live**/**lives** next door?
9 Why **you were lying**/**were you lying** on the floor?
10 We **played**/**were playing** chess when the phone rang.

10

B Complete the sentences with *be*, *have* or *have got* in the correct form.

1 Where _____ you last night?
2 He _____ a well-paid job. He works in a bank.
3 _____ you _____ a good meal last night?
4 _____ the house _____ a big garden?
5 '_____ you ill?' 'No, I _____ not. I feel fine.'

5

C Complete the sentences with verbs in the present simple or continuous.

1 Look at my stomach! It (get) ~~is~~ getting bigger!
2 '(you/understand) do you understand Japanese?' 'No, I d'ont.'
3 'Where (he/come) does he come from?' 'Taiwan, I (think) _____'
4 'Excuse me, you (sit) are sitting in my place.' 'Oh, I'm sorry.'
5 'Which hotel (they/stay) they are staying at?' 'The Ritz. (you/know) do you know it?'

5

D Write the sentence with the adverb in the correct position.

1 We finish work at midday. (hardly ever) We never [hardly] finish work at midday
2 Does she eat here? (ever) Does she never eat here?
3 I don't come home tired. (every evening) _____
4 Was he a good singer? (always) _____
5 They went skiing. (rarely) _____

5

E Complete the sentences with verbs in the past simple or continuous.

1 (you/stand) ~~You~~ *you* were Standing here when the accident (happen) happened ?

2 While I (visit) was visiting her, she (introduce) introduced me to her brother.

3 We (meet) met them while they (travel) were travelling in Russia.

4 I (not/like) I didn't like him when he (be) was a child a child.

5 She (have) had a bad dream when she (wake) was waking up.

[ ] **5**

F Complete the question. Use the information in brackets.

1 '................................ *Hamlet*?' 'Shakespeare did.' (Shakespeare wrote *Hamlet*.)

2 '................................ that dress?' 'In Moscow.' (I bought it in Moscow.)

3 '................................ dinner?' 'My husband is.' (My husband's cooking dinner.)

4 '................................?' 'The best one.' (The best team won.)

5 '................................ here?' 'Four other people.' (Four other people live here.)

6 '................................?' 'Pasta.' (She ate pasta.)

7 '................................ pasta?' 'She did.' (She ate pasta.)

8 '................................?' 'Nothing.' (Nothing happened.)

9 '................................?' 'Arabic.' (They're studying Arabic.)

10 '................................ to Nice?' 'The 6.00 pm.' (The 6.00 pm train goes to Nice.)

[ ] **10**

G Correct the mistakes.

1 Is <u>difficult your job</u>? ....

2 We <u>didn't have got</u> much sun here yesterday. ....

3 'Did you have a swim?' No, I <u>didn't have</u>.' ....

4 My brother's <u>liveing</u> here at the moment. ....

5 This shop <u>sell</u> cheese. ....

6 A lot of people <u>is liking</u> fast food. ....

7 Do you <u>live usually</u> in New York? ....

8 He <u>didn't knew</u> the answer. ....

9 Who <u>did say</u> that? ....

10 When we went out, the sun <u>already shone</u>. ....

[ ] **10**

TOTAL [ ] **50**

11 A city in the north

a/an or the?

We use *a/an* when:
we talk about something new. There's **a** woman at the door.
we say what something is/what job someone does. Their new film is **a** comedy.
we describe something. It's **a** lovely day. What **a** good idea!

We use *the* when:
we are talking about something for the second time. I had **a** cake and **an** ice-cream.
The ice-cream was delicious.
there is only one. **The** moon is very bright tonight. **The** longest river in **the** world.
It is clear what we are talking about from the situation: Pass me **the** milk, please.

Expressions: *play the piano, go to the airport/the shops, go to the doctor, in the south*

A Underline the correct answer.

1   Sorry, I can't stop! I'm going to **an/the** airport.

2   Do you know 'The God of Small Things'?
It's **a/the** great novel about India.

3   Who's **an/the** author?

4   What's **a/the** weather like in India this time of year?

5   Does your friend play **a/the** musical instrument?

6   Yes, he plays **a/the** sitar.

7   What's **a/the** name of **a/the** main river that runs through Calcutta?

8   **A/The** Hooghly.

B Complete this part of a tourist guide with *a/an* or *the*.

Agra is (1) _a_ city in (2) _the_ north of India. It is famous for its Mogul architecture, especially (3) _the_ Taj Mahal, which is (4) _a_ beautiful monument and one of (5) _the_ most famous buildings in (6) _the_ world. (7) _the_ monument was built by Shah Jahan in (8) _the_ 17th century. It has (9) _a_ wonderful dome, which is decorated with designs of plants and flowers. (10) _the_ designs are common in Islamic architecture. Visitors to Agra can get there by train or plane. (11) _the_ airport is only 7km from (12) _the_ city centre.

12 I'm taking my test tomorrow

A Underline the correct answer.

1   I'm hungry. I think **I'll have**/**I'm having** lunch.

2   Sorry, I can't come with you. **I'll meet**/**I'm meeting** a customer in an hour.

3   Please **will you**/**are you going to** book me a table at the Riverside Restaurant.

4   Don't tell Greg where I'm going! **He'll tell**/**He's telling** the whole office.

5   **Shall I**/**Am I going to** organise your trip to Poland while you're at lunch?

6   I've heard **Danuta'll**/**Danuta's going to** have a baby. Do you know when?

7   She **won't listen**/**'s not listening** to me. She thinks she knows everything.

B Complete the email with *shall/'ll* + verb or the present continuous.

From: Joanna Miles, PA
To: Serge Franck, Marketing Director
Subject: Visit to Poland

Hope you had a good lunch!

I've made some arrangements for your trip. You *'re catching* (1 catch) the 6.30 am flight from Heathrow on Tuesday, so you will get (2 get) to Warsaw early. I've phoned Danuta and she says she 'll be (3 be) at the airport to meet you. You will not doing (4 not/do) anything in the morning, so you 'r having (5 have) time to relax. You are staying (6 stay) at the Sofitel Hotel – it's close to our office and very comfortable. At 2.00 pm, you 'll meet (7 meet) the sales team. Unfortunately, Konrad .... (8 not/be) there, but he's promised he .... (9 take) you out to dinner in the evening.

.... (10 book/l) you a return flight for early Wednesday morning? Let me know.

Joanna

C Complete the dialogues. Which country is each pair talking about?

1 Bilgen: They don't speak Spanish there!
   Chikako: I know. I've decided *I'm going to learn* a little Portuguese before I go.
   (I'll learn/I'm going to learn)

   Brazil

2 Chen: It can get to –30°C at night sometimes.
   Vibeke: Yes, but I'm sure .... cold. The houses are very well-heated.
   (you won't be/you're not being)
   ....

3 Saifiya: .... you a hotel near the pyramids?
   Crispin: Yes, please, for Tuesday night, after my trip down the Nile.
   (Will I book /Shall I book)
   ....

4 Iacomo: Do you know it's where they invented surfing?
   Constanta: Yes, ... to a competition there next year.
   (I'll go/I'm going)
   ....

5 Majeed: When you get there, ... local dishes or western food?
   Roza: Local dishes! I want to try some raw fish!
   (are you going to eat/are you eating)
   ....

6 Nairi: At the moment it's the rainy season.
   Jakome: Really? .... an umbrella! What about the food? Is it always spicy?
   (I'll take/I'm going to take)
   ....

13 We have to go

have to

Necessary: We **have to** book. They're usually very busy
Not necessary: We **don't have to** book. You can always get a table.

Past and future forms:

Positive		Question	
He **had to** He'**ll have to**	go.	**Did** he **have to** **Will** he **have to**	go?
Negative		Answer	
He **didn't have to** He **won't have to**	go.	Yes, he **did.** he **will.**	No, he **didn't**. he **won't**.

A Complete the sentences with the correct form of *have to* in the present.

1 You *don't have to find* (find) a place to stay.

2 You _____ (pay) for the first round of golf every day.

3 You _____ (buy) any golf balls.

4 You _____ (take) your own golf clubs.

5 You _____ (book) before 1st December.

GOLF BREAKS

Included in the price
✓ full hotel accommodation
✓ first round of golf every day
✓ 50 golf balls
✗ golf clubs

Last day for booking:
1st December.

B Complete the questions and answers with *have to* in the present, past (for last time) or future (for next time).

1 (*Do you have to play* (you/play) in groups of four?)   (Yes, you *do.*)

2 (_____ (Nadia/wear) golf shoes last time?)   (Yes, she _____.)

3 (_____ (Rob/play) in the junior competition next time?)   (No, he _____.)

4 (_____ (Lois/have) golf lessons next time?)   (No, she _____.)

5 (_____ (you/buy) new golf trousers last time?)   (No, I _____.)

6 (When _____ (I/book)?)   (Now! It's very popular.)

14 I like apples

A Underline the correct answer.

A We're going to (1) <u>**Japan**</u>/the Japan in (2) <u>**September**</u>/the September.

B Oh, are you? I lived in Japan for a while. I went to (3) **Kyoto University/the Kyoto University**. (4) **Kyoto/The Kyoto** is a great city. Did you know, it used to be the capital of Japan until (5) **19th century/the 19th century**?

A No, that's interesting. How big is it?

B Not too big. You can explore most of the city (6) **on foot/on the foot**. There are hundreds of (7) **temples/the temples** and (8) **lovely gardens/the lovely gardens** to visit. Do you speak (9) **Japanese/the Japanese**?

A No, I don't.

B Never mind. (10) **The Japanese/Japanese** are very good at speaking (11) **English/the English**.

B Write *the* or X (nothing) in the gaps.

1 These days (1) __X__ Japanese cooking is familiar around the world. In many countries outside (2) _____ Japan, people eat sashimi, which is (3) _____ raw fish, or tempura, which is fish or (4) _____ vegetables cooked in (5) _____ oil.

2 Going out for (1) _____ dinner is one of (2) _____ greatest pleasures of (3) _____ Japanese life and (4) _____ Tokyo is one of (5) _____ world's greatest cities for (6) _____ restaurants. Many first-time visitors to (7) _____ city are surprised by the variety of (8) _____ Japanese food.

3 Many restaurants have plastic (1) _____ copies of their dishes in (2) _____ front window, or a colour photograph on (3) _____ menu. This is for people who can't speak (4) _____ Japanese. The quality of the food inside (5) _____ restaurant is always excellent.

15 We must hurry

should/must

	Positive	Negative
I/He/She/We/You/They	**should** go.	**shouldn't** watch.
I/He/She/We/You/They	**must** hurry.	**mustn't** touch.

We use:
should and *shouldn't* to give advice. You **should** take your camera. You **shouldn't** eat so quickly.
must when something's necessary. I **must** go to the bank.
mustn't when it's necessary not to do something. You **mustn't** copy in the exam.

ⓘ *must* is stronger than *should*

A **Match the signs with the sentences and complete with the correct form of *should* or *must*.**

A 15

D DANGER
NO SWIMMING

B FORMAL DRESS

E CAUTION WET FLOOR

C MEMBERS ONLY

F RESERVED

_F_ 1 We *should* book a table next time. (should)

_D_ 2 You *mustn't* swim at this beach today! (must)

_A_ 3 Lucy *shouldn't* watch that film. She's only twelve. (should)

_C_ 4 I'm sorry, you *must* leave immediately. You're not a member. (must)

_B_ 5 You *should* wear your new suit. (should)

_E_ 6 We *shouldn't* walk on this. Someone's cleaning it. (should)

B **Complete these rules from the Highway Code with the correct form of *should* or *must*.**

1 You *mustn't* overtake on a corner.

2 People .... use a pedestrian crossing where possible. It's much safer.

3 You .... stop when you see this sign. **STOP**

4 You .... drive over 40 miles per hour. **(40)**

5 You .... use your lights in a tunnel when you see this sign.

6 You .... go down a road when you see this sign.

16 A lot of information

Quantity

Countable nouns		Uncountable nouns	
We've got There are	some computers. a lot of envelopes. plenty of chairs. (= a lot) a few tables. a couple of computers. (= 2) several clocks. (= 3+)	We've got There is	some coffee. a lot of information. plenty of time. a little water. (= not much)
There aren't We haven't got	any office diaries. a lot of telephones. many desks.	There isn't We haven't got	any paper. a lot of machinery. much money.
How many fax machines are there?		How much information is there?	
Not many./None./A couple./A few.		Not much./A little./A lot.	

A Look at the list of office equipment. Underline the correct answer.

GENERAL ELECTRONICS

new equipment	✓
laptop computers	2
old machinery	in one room
desk lamps	25
modern printers	8
new telephones	18

1 a/some new equipment.
2 a little/a couple of computers
3 any/some old machinery
4 a few/a lot of desk lamps
5 a couple of/several modern printers
6 plenty of/a little new telephones

B Look at the list and write sentences using a phrase from the box.

> any   a couple of   a few
> a lot of   ~~plenty of~~   some

cupboards	18
security cameras	2
expensive furniture	in one room
shelves	250
fax paper	✗
filing cabinets	4

1 There are plenty of cupboards.
2 There are a couple of security cameras.
3 There are a few expensive
4 There are many shelves.
5 There isn't have any fax paper.
6 There are several filing

C Write the correct answer in the gap.

DESIGN YOUR OWN WEBSITE

- Include (1) (a few/plenty of/several) _plenty of_ useful information but don't use too (2) (many/much/a few) .... words.
- Don't make (3) (some/any/much) .... spelling mistakes!
- Add (4) (a little/any/a few) .... pictures but not (5) (any/a lot of/several) .... them. (6) (Many/A little/Much) .... computers are very slow.
- You can use (7) (a few/a little/much) .... music but not too (8) (plenty/much/many) ....
- You can have (9) (a couple of/plenty of/much) .... advertisements but not (10) (plenty/many/much) .... more. People don't like (11) (many/several/a lot of) .... advertising.
- Get the right designer. Designers cost (12) (many/a lot of/several) .... money!

D Complete the questions and answers about designing a website.

1 'How _much_ information do you need?'   ' _Plenty._ '

2 'How .... words do you use?'   ' .... '

3 'How .... pictures do you have?'   ' .... '

4 'How .... music do you use?'   ' .... '

5 'How .... advertisements can you have?'   ' .... '

E Complete the sentences about your favourite website. Say how much/many.

1 It _hasn't got any/has got plenty of_ advertising.

2 It .... advertisements.

3 It .... information.

4 There .... pictures.

5 There .... music.

6 It ....

17 She's just won

Present perfect			▶▶ Irregular verbs page 61.
Positive	I/You/We/They**'ve** (**have**) He/She/It**'s** (**has**)		finished.
Negative	I/You/We/They He/She/It	**haven't** (**have not**) **hasn't** (**has not**)	
Question	**Have** **Has**	I/you/we/they he/she/it	finished?

I've worked here for three years. (= I work here now.)
He's just left. (= He's not here now.)
Have you (ever) been to India? (= In your life up to now.)

! We don't use the present perfect if we say <u>when</u> something happened in the past. NOT
~~We have met him yesterday~~

A Write the verbs in these news stories in the present perfect.

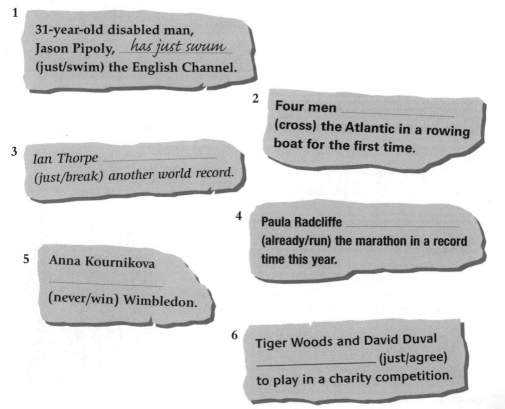

1
31-year-old disabled man,
Jason Pipoly, *has just swum*
(just/swim) the English Channel.

2 Four men _____
(cross) the Atlantic in a rowing
boat for the first time.

3 *Ian Thorpe* _____
(just/break) another world record.

4 Paula Radcliffe _____
(already/run) the marathon in a record
time this year.

5 Anna Kournikova
_____
(never/win) Wimbledon.

6 Tiger Woods and David Duval
_____ (just/agree)
to play in a charity competition.

B Complete the sentences with the correct form of the verb in brackets. Use the past simple or present perfect.

1 **A**: Have you ever ___won___ (win) a big competition?

   B: Yes, I _have_ . I ___won___ (win) a holiday to the Maldives last year.

2 **A**: Have you ever _____ (break) your leg?

   B: Yes, I _____ . I _____ (break) it on a skiing holiday two years ago.

3 **A**: Have you ever _____ (make) a really bad financial decision?

   B: No, I _____ All my life. I _____ (be) very careful with money.

4 **A**: Have you ever (be) _____ really ill?

   B: Yes, I _____ . I _____ (be) in hospital for three weeks once.

5 **A**: Have you ever _____ (lose) all the data on your computer?

   B: No, I _____ . I _____ (always/make) a back-up copy.

C Answer the questions in C for you. Use the present perfect and/or the past simple.

1 _Yes, I have. I won the lottery last year!_ OR _No, I haven't._

2 _____

3 _____

4 _____

5 _____

D Write the verbs in the present perfect or the past simple.

A Happy Couple

The film stars Paul Newman and Joanne Woodward first (1 meet) ___met___ in 1952 and (2 marry) _____ in 1958. They (3 be) _____ together now for over 40 years. In his career Paul (4 appear) _____ in many classic films, such as 'The Hustler', and in 2002 he (5 play) _____ a Mafia gangster in 'The Road to Perdition'. A few years ago he (6 start) _____ a very successful food company. Paul (7 always/be) _____ a generous man and (8 decide) _____ at the time to give all the company's profits to a children's charity. Throughout her life, Joanne (9 also/have) _____ a lot of work – in the theatre, on TV and in the cinema. She says that their time together (10 not/always/be) _____ easy. She (11 hate) _____ their film star life when the children (12 be) _____ young, but now she says she and Paul have a quiet and happy family life together away from Hollywood.

18 Do you want to go out?

	Verb	+ verb-*ing*		Verb	+ *to* + verb
He	enjoys	paint**ing**.	She	decided	**to** leave.
They've	stopped	talk**ing**.	I	promise	**to** phone.
Other verbs: *enjoy, can't help, hate, like, don't mind, suggest*			Other verbs: *forget, hope, need, 'd like, wait, want*		

ⓘ We normally use *mind* in the negative form and question form. I didn't **mind** help**ing**.
Did you **mind** do**ing** all that work?

She **can't help** shout**ing**. (= She can't stop herself from shouting.)

A Complete the sentences. Use verbs from the advert with *-ing* or *to*.

1 Do you enjoy _listening_ to live jazz?

2 When do they finish _____ meals?

3 Don't forget _____ early.

4 Do we need _____ our tickets at the box office?

5 They suggest _____ them online.

6 I don't mind _____ smart clothes for one night!

NEW ORLEANS JAZZ CLUB
Listen to the best live jazz in town.
Meals served until 10pm. Arrive early for tables by the window.
Buy tickets at the box office or book online.
Dress: wear smart clothes (no jeans)

B Complete the letter with the correct form of the verbs.

Last night I promised (1) _to take_ (take) Carmen out for her birthday and she said she'd like (2) _____ (go) for a meal at the jazz club. Normally I hate (3) _____ (eat) in places like that but the food there is very good. We wanted (4) _____ (sit) outside but it didn't stop (5) _____ (rain) all evening.
I forgot (6) _____ (tell) you that Carmen and I are hoping (7) _____ (get) married soon. She's waiting (8) _____ (hear) about a new job before we decide on a day.
I can't help (9) _____ (feel) a bit worried about getting married, though. I like my freedom!!

C Complete the sentences about you. Use verb + *-ing* or *to* + verb.

1 I hope _to get a new job soon._

2 I'm going to stop _____

3 I've decided _____

4 I usually forget _____

5 I'm waiting _____

6 I've promised _____

19 If you write to us

Present simple	Present
If I **need** extra money,	I **work** overtime. (It happens every time.)
Present simple	Imperative
If it**'s** cold later tonight,	**take** your coat with you.
Present simple	Future
If you **don't eat** now,	you**'ll feel** hungry later. (An event in the future.)

ⓘ When the *if* clause comes second you don't use a comma. I **work** overtime
if I **need** extra money.

ⓘ We can also use *when* instead of *if* for things we know are going to happen.
When I **see** John, I**'ll tell** him you called. (I'm definitely going to see him.)
If I **see** John, I**'ll tell** him you called. (I'm possibly going to see him.)

A Match the sentence parts.

1 If I don't have much breakfast, __b__

2 If I don't get any exercise, _____

3 If the weather's nice, _____

4 If I feel tired when I get home, _____

5 If I get thirsty in the middle of the night, _____

6 If there's nothing on TV, _____

a I have lunch outside

b I get hungry by 10.00

c I put on weight

d I relax in a hot bath

e I read a book

f I drink a glass of water

B Continue the sentence for you.

1 I get a headache if *I drink a lot of coffee.*

2 I put on weight if _____

3 I get a cold if _____

4 I feel tired if _____

5 I watch TV if _____

C Put the verbs in these sentences in the correct form.

EUROTUNNEL – *TOURIST INFORMATION*

1 If you (buy) *buy* your tickets before next March, we (offer) *'ll offer* you cheaper tickets.

2 If you (arrive) _____ without a ticket, we (put) _____ you on the earliest train.

3 If you (want) _____ to buy some wine and cheese, you (find) _____ shops at the terminal.

4 When you (get) _____ on the train, just (relax) _____ in your car for the whole journey!

5 If you (need) _____ petrol, you (see) _____ a petrol station on your left.

6 When you (arrive) _____ in England, (not/forget) _____ to drive on the left!

20 He couldn't sing

can/could

Present	Past
I **can** swim.	I **couldn't** swim.
He **can't** drive.	He **couldn't** drive.
Can you speak Spanish?	**Could** you speak Spanish?
Yes, I **can**. /No, I **can't**.	Yes, I **could**. /No, I **couldn't**.

ⓘ We also use *can/can't, could/couldn't* to say that something is or isn't possible.
You **can** get a bus or go by taxi. I **couldn't** get there by metro.

A Underline the correct form for you.

Now:

1 I **can**/can't swim.
2 I **can**/**can't** drive.
3 I **can**/**can't** ride a bicycle.
4 I **can**/**can't** speak English.
5 I **can**/**can't** play the violin.

Fifteen years ago:

1 I **could**/**couldn't** swim.
2 I **could**/**couldn't** drive.
3 I **could**/**couldn't** ride a bicycle.
4 I **could**/**couldn't** speak English.
5 I **could**/**couldn't** play the violin.

B Complete the sentences with *can, can't, could* or *couldn't*.

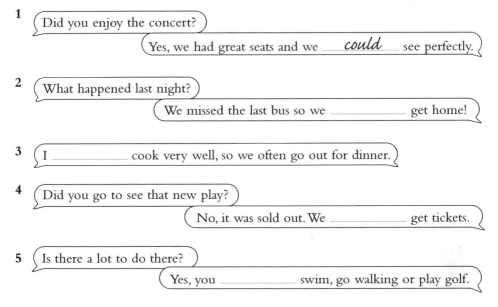

1 Did you enjoy the concert?
Yes, we had great seats and we ___*could*___ see perfectly.

2 What happened last night?
We missed the last bus so we _____ get home!

3 I _____ cook very well, so we often go out for dinner.

4 Did you go to see that new play?
No, it was sold out. We _____ get tickets.

5 Is there a lot to do there?
Yes, you _____ swim, go walking or play golf.

Test 2 (Units 11–20)

A Circle the correct form.

1 Who's **a/the** man in the car?

2 '**Shall I/Am I** going to shut the window?' 'Yes, please.'

3 **Do you have to drive/Have you to drive** on the left?

4 He speaks **good Russian/the good Russian**.

5 I don't think you **should/must** wear that coat.

6 There's only **a few/a little** milk.

7 He**'s stayed/stayed** with us last week.

8 I stopped **smoking/to smoke** a year ago. I feel much better.

9 If she**'ll get/gets** to work late, she'll lose her job.

10 I **can't/couldn't** drive two years ago.

10

B Write *a, the* or X (nothing).

1 Where's .... ticket?

2 *Hamlet* is .... wonderful play.

3 She plays .... saxophone very well.

4 In general, do you think .... women are .... good drivers?

5 I went to Tokyo by .... train.

5

C Write the correct form of the verbs.

1 If it (snow) .... this winter, we (go) .... skiing. (present simple or *'ll?*)

2 He's a friend. I (know) .... him for a long time. (past simple or present perfect?)

3 '(we/watch) .... a video?' 'No, I'm too tired.' (*shall* or *will?*)

4 If I (see) .... her tomorrow, I (ask) .... her. (present simple or *'ll?*)

5 I (lose) .... my keys. I can't find them. (past simple or present perfect?)

5

D Correct the mistakes.

1 I'd love to see you but we'<u>ll go</u> away for the weekend. ....

2 <u>Have you had</u> a holiday last year? ....

3 <u>Shall</u> you lend me a pen, please? ....

4 'I haven't got any money.' 'OK, I'<u>m going to</u> pay.' ....

5 If we <u>won't</u> leave now, we'll miss the plane. ....

5

34

E Complete the sentences with *have to* in the correct form.

1 '(you) _____ get up early yesterday morning?' 'Yes, I did.'

2 She _____ see a doctor last night. She had stomach ache.

3 I'm getting a car next week. I _____ walk to work any more after that!

4 We _____ wait long for the bus. It arrived very quickly.

5 When you get your new house next year, (you) _____ buy new furniture?

5

F Complete the sentences with the correct form of *should* or *must*.

1 He's broken his leg. Quick! We _____ phone the doctor.

2 You look tired. You _____ stay up so late every night!

3 You _____ forget your passport when you go to the airport tomorrow.

4 I'm going to Poland for a holiday. Do you think I _____ learn to speak some Polish?

5 Take care of these important papers. You _____ lose them!

5

G Write the correct alternative.

1 How _____ information do you need? (many/a lot of/much)

2 I've got _____ questions to ask you. (any/a little/several)

3 'How _____ people are there?' (some/many/much)
'_____' (A little./A few.)

4 You've made _____ mistakes. (any/a lot/a lot of)

5 Is there _____ milk? (any/a couple of/several)

5

H Write the verb in the correct form.

1 He needs (tell) _____ you something.

2 Don't forget (send) _____ us a postcard.

3 I can't help (laugh) _____ .

4 Do you mind (get) _____ up early tomorrow morning?

5 She promised (help) _____ me.

5

I Write *can, can't, could, couldn't* in the gaps.

1 Last night I was tired but I _____ sleep.

2 I _____ work with all this noise!

3 When she was young, she _____ sing beautifully.

4 Have you seen my shoes? I _____ find them.

5 I love this place. You _____ really relax here.

5

TOTAL **50**

21 I'll see you when you get back

when/as soon as/after

	Present simple	Present simple
When/	I get up in the mornings,	I have a shower. (It happens every time.)
As soon as/	Present simple	Future
After	I get to New York next week,	I'll hire a car. (An event in the future.)
		I'm going to look for a job.

as soon as = at the same time or a very short time after.

! We use the present simple for future time after *when/as soon as/after*.
NOT ~~When I will get to New York, ...~~

A Write the verbs in the present simple.

Andrea works in TV. She's a TV foreign correspondent. As soon as she (1) _arrives_ (arrive) in a country, she (2) .... (find) people to interview for her story. It is often very dangerous work, and when she (3) .... (get) a few moments to relax, she (4) .... (like) to go shopping and buy something for her flat in England, like a carpet or a painting. When she (5) .... (arrive) in England, Andrea (6) .... (return) to her flat in Notting Hill in London. Every day after she (7) .... (get up), she (8) .... (phone) the office to find out about her next job. It's very tiring work so as soon as she (9) .... (have) a holiday she (10) .... (get on) her boat with some friends and (11) .... (go) down the River Thames.

B These are the producer's instructions for Andrea's next job. Write the verbs in the correct form.

1 When you ....._get to_..... (get to) Downing Street, you're going to interview the Prime Minister.

2 The cameraman .... (meet) you when you .... (arrive).

3 As soon as you .... (finish) the interview, a taxi will take you back to the studio.

4 We'll edit the film after you .... (get back).

5 When we .... (finish) the film, I .... (arrange) your trip to Afghanistan.

6 Will you call me as soon as your plane .... (land) in Kabul?

22 What's she like?

like

What's		Esther		She's very friendly.
What	was	your car		It was big but very old.
What	are	the grapes	like?	They're lovely and sweet.
What	were	the teachers		They were very mean.

ⓘ **'What is** Esther **like**?' (Tell me something about her.) 'She's very shy.'
'How is Esther?' (Asking about her health.) 'She's not very well.'

A Match the questions with the answers.

1 What's Natsuko like? __c__   **a** Very well. She's happy here.

2 What sports does she like? _____   **b** She's lovely, like Natsuko.

3 How is she? _____   **c** Quite young and very nice.

4 What food does she like? _____   **d** Swimming and playing tennis.

5 What's her sister like? _____   **e** Japanese food, of course!

B Natsuko has just come back from an interview. Write her husband's questions with *What ... like*? Use the words in the box.

the office   the computers   the job
the money   the other people   ~~the manager~~

COMPUTER ENGINEERS WANTED.

1 _What was the manager like?_   'He was very friendly.'

2 _____   'It's quite good. About $2000 a week.'

3 _____   'They were very helpful.'

4 _____   'I don't know. It might be difficult.'

5 _____   'It's modern but a bit small.'

6 _____   'Very new and very fast.'

C Your friend has just come back from holiday. Ask questions with *What ... like*?

1 (the hotel) _What was the hotel like?_

2 (the food) _____

3 (the people) _____

4 (the flight) _____

5 (the beaches) _____

23 It's a bigger room

	Adjective	Comparative
One syllable	thin hard dry	thin**ner** hard**er** dri**er**
Two syllables ending in -y	dirty friendly	dirt**ier** friendl**ier**
Two or more syllables	intelligent popular	**more** intelligent **more** popular
Irregular	good bad far	**better** **worse** **further** (farther)

! Spelling: nice → nicer; big → bigger

ⓘ well → **better**   badly → **worse**   much/many/a lot of → **more**

A Write sentences comparing the hotels.

		Rooms	Facilities	Price	
The Crown	1900	31	Car park	£85	**
The Star	2001	125	Gym/ Indoor pool	£125	****

1 *The Star has got more rooms than The Crown.* (a lot of rooms)
2 *The Crown is older than The Star.* (old)
3 .... (small)
4 .... (a lot of facilities)
5 .... (modern)
6 .... (expensive)
7 .... (cheap)
8 .... (good)

B Use comparative3 forms to complete the memo.

Memo

TO: John Potts   **FROM:** Gillian Franks
Re: Hotel reservation for overseas visitors

I went to see both hotels. The Star is a (1) ..... *bigger* ..... (big) hotel but I thought The Crown was
(2) .... (interesting) and (3) .... (comfortable). The rooms were
(4) .... (bright) and there was a nice, big fire in the lounge. The Star is much
(5) .... (new) than The Crown, but inside it was much (6) .... (dirty).
The Crown is in a (7) .... (good) location, because it is (8) .... (near) the
centre of town, but it is much (9) .... (noisy) than The Star. In my view, The Crown is a
(10) .... (attractive) hotel and I would recommend it for our visitors.

24 If I was the manager, I'd ...

	Past simple	would + verb
Positive	**If** I **was** the manager,	**I'd (would)** buy a new house.
Negative	**If** I **didn't speak** Spanish,	I **wouldn't work** in Mexico.
Question	**If** you **moved** to China,	**would** you **get** a job there?

ⓘ When the *if* clause comes second, you don't use a comma. **Would** you **get** a job in China **if** you **lived** there?

If I **was** the manager, ... (= I'm not the manager.) The situation is not real.
If I **didn't speak** Spanish, ... (= I speak Spanish.)

A Underline the correct answer.

1 If I **find/found** a wallet in the street, I would take it to a police station.
2 If I **don't like/didn't like** a girl friend's new hairstyle, I would tell her.
3 I **will/would** tell the bank if there was too much money in my bank account.
4 If a shop assistant **gives/gave** me too much change, I would give it back.
5 If I saw someone cheating in an exam, I **will/would** complain.

B Write the verbs in the past then write questions with *would*.

ARE YOU HONEST?
Imagine these situations.

1 If you *broke* (break) an expensive vase in a shop, *would you tell* (you/tell) the manager?
2 If you _____ (find) someone's personal diary, _____ (you/read) it?
3 _____ (you/say) something if a waiter _____ (forget) to write an item on the bill?
4 If your child _____ (take) a toy from a shop by mistake, _____ (you/return) it?
5 _____ (you/leave) your phone number if you _____ (hit) a car in a car park?
6 If someone at work _____ (be) taking printer paper home, _____ (you/tell) the boss?

C What would you do in the situations in B?

1 I *would/wouldn't tell* _____ the manager.
2 I _____ it.
3 I _____ something.
4 I _____ it.
5 I _____ my phone number.
6 I _____ the boss.

25 The best restaurant

	Adjective	Superlative
One syllable	small rich	(the) smallest (the) richest
Two syllables ending in –y	easy early	(the) easiest (the) earliest
Two or more syllables	comfortable	(the) most comfortable
Irregular	good bad far	(the) best (the) worst (the) furthest (farthest)

A Complete the sentences comparing the restaurants.

	Friendly atmosphere	Fast service	Good food	Interesting menu	Price
Enzo's	4	2	3	4	£££££
Bistro	3	3	5	3	££
Curry House	5	5	4	5	£££

(5 = excellent, 1 = poor; £££££ = high, £ = low)

1 The Curry House has _the friendliest_ atmosphere.
2 The Bistro has _____ prices.
3 The Curry House has _____ service.
4 The Bistro has _____ food.
5 Enzo's has _____ prices.
6 The Curry House has _____ menu.
7 Enzo's has _____ food.

B Use superlative forms to complete these restaurant reviews.

1
The Terraco Italia restaurant is at the top of the _tallest_ (tall) building
in Sao Paulo and offers the _____ (good) view of the city after
sunset. One of its _____ (famous) visitors was Queen Elizabeth II.

2
The Bellevue is one of Prague's _____ (fine) formal
dining rooms and has the _____ (high) quality food
and service. It's not the _____ (cheap) restaurant
in town, but it is one of the _____ (busy).

3
The Erakor in Vanuatu is one of the _____ (romantic)
restaurants on the South Pacific islands. The _____ (popular)
day is Sundays when people eat their lunches on the beach.

26 I like people who are friendly

Defining relative clauses

who/that (for people)

I saw the man	**who/that**	lives next door. (I saw the man. He lives next door.)

that/which (for things and animals)

I need the key	**that/which**	opens the front door. (I need the key. It opens the front door.)

where (for places)

This is the house	**where**	I was born.

when (for time)

That was the day	**when**	I lost my luggage.

A Underline the correct answer.

MY LIKES AND DISLIKES

1 I like people **who**/**which** are polite.
2 I don't like people **when**/**who** get angry a lot.
3 I like days **who**/**when** there is a lot to do.
4 I like cars **that**/**who** don't use much petrol.
5 I like books **when**/**which** are easy to read.
6 I don't like restaurants **that**/**where** they play loud music.

B Complete the sentences in A for you.

1 I like people _who can sing._ (work hard? can sing?)
2 I don't like people _____ (rude? noisy?)
3 I like days _____ (weather/good? we go home early?)
4 I like cars _____ (easy to drive? go fast?)
5 I like books _____ (amusing? serious?)
6 I don't like restaurants _____ (service/bad? the waiters/rude?)

C Join the sentences with *who, that, which, where* or *when*.

1 Michelle has a husband. He laughs a lot. _Michelle has a husband who laughs a lot._
2 He wears jeans. They don't fit. _____
3 She has a brother. He sends them money. _____
4 They have a dog. It hates loud noises. _____
5 They love weekends. They can be together then. _____

27 London isn't as big as Tokyo

		as + adjective	+ as	
Ilia	is	tall	as	Aref. (They are the same height.)
Mikel	isn't	heavy		Pavel. (Pavel is heavier.)

ⓘ Mikel is **almost as** heavy **as** Pavel. Mikel is**n't quite as** heavy **as** Pavel. (There is a small difference. Pavel is a little heavier.)

A Compare these islands and then complete the sentences with *as ... as* and one of the adjectives in brackets.

	Population	Area (sq km)	Average temperature	Average rainfall (mm)
CUBA	11,184,023	110,860	24°C	1,375
MALTA	397,499	316	18.5°C	510
TAIWAN	22,191,00	36,000	22.25°C	2,500

Cuba

Malta

Taiwan

1 Taiwan *isn't as large as* .... Cuba. (large/small)

2 The population of Cuba .... the population of Malta. (large/small)

3 Malta .... Cuba or Taiwan. (wet/dry)

4 Taiwan .... Cuba. (almost hot/almost cool)

5 Taiwan .... Cuba. (quite hot/quite cool)

6 Cuba .... Malta. (wet/dry)

7 The population of Malta .... the population of Taiwan. (large/small)

B Compare these things. Use the adjective in brackets.

1 (jazz/opera) *Jazz is/isn't as good as opera. (OR Opera is/isn't as good as jazz.)* (good)

2 (fruit/meat) .... (healthy)

3 (motor-racing/boxing) .... (dangerous)

4 (snakes/spiders) .... (horrible)

5 (men/women) .... (intelligent)

6 (Einstein/Shakespeare) .... (important)

7 (history/science) .... (interesting)

28 Pleased to meet you

	adjective	+ *to*-infinitive
I'm	**pleased**	**to see** you.
He was	**amazed**	**to get** the job.
His writing is (not)	**difficult**	**to read**.

ⓘ We can use *It* with some adjectives + *to*-infinitive. **It's important to drive** carefully. **It's stupid to spend** all your money.

A Complete the sentences with verbs from the box in the correct form.

> get ~~see~~ understand walk win

1 I was amazed ___*to see*___ Gwyneth Paltrow in a British film. She was good!
2 I think Michael Caine is certain .... an Oscar.
3 The plot wasn't very easy .... It was too complicated.
4 The film was scary. I was afraid .... home afterwards!
5 We were disappointed not .... tickets for the Bond film.

B Complete this email, using the adjectives and verbs in brackets.

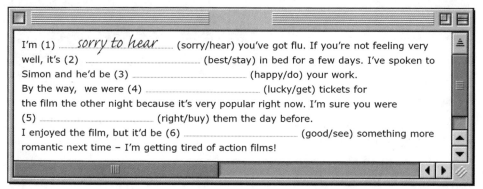

I'm (1) ___*sorry to hear*___ (sorry/hear) you've got flu. If you're not feeling very
well, it's (2) .... (best/stay) in bed for a few days. I've spoken to
Simon and he'd be (3) .... (happy/do) your work.
By the way, we were (4) .... (lucky/get) tickets for
the film the other night because it's very popular right now. I'm sure you were
(5) .... (right/buy) them the day before.
I enjoyed the film, but it'd be (6) .... (good/see) something more
romantic next time – I'm getting tired of action films!

C Write sentences about what you think in the positive or negative.

1 ___*Romantic novels are (not) very exciting to read.*___ (exciting/read)
2 .... (difficult/learn)
3 .... (easy/understand)
4 .... (impossible/remember)
5 .... (nice/eat)

29 He used to play tennis

used to

Positive		I/He/She/We/	**used to**	live here.
Negative		You/They	**didn't use to**	
Question	**Did**		**use to**	live here?
Answer	Yes,	I/he/she/we/	**did.**	
	No,	you/they	**didn't.**	

I **used to** live in Dublin. (In the past. I don't live there now.)
I **used to** go out every night. (In the past. I don't go out every night now.)

A Complete the sentences with *used to* + the verb. Can you match the sentences with the photos?

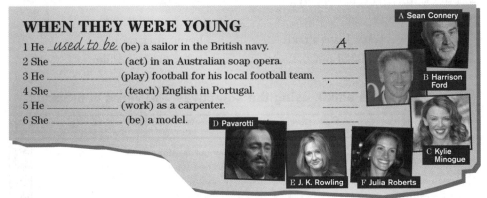

WHEN THEY WERE YOUNG

1 He _used to be_ (be) a sailor in the British navy. _____ A

2 She _____ (act) in an Australian soap opera. _____

3 He _____ (play) football for his local football team. _____

4 She _____ (teach) English in Portugal. _____

5 He _____ (work) as a carpenter. _____

6 She _____ (be) a model. _____

A Sean Connery
B Harrison Ford
C Kylie Minogue
D Pavarotti
E J. K. Rowling
F Julia Roberts

B Make questions about when you were young with *used to*.

1 (families/spend more time together) _Did families use to spend more time together?_

2 (women/stay at home more) _____

3 (children/read more) _____

4 (you/listen to the radio a lot) _____

5 (men and women/get married earlier) _____

C Answer the questions in B about life when you were a child.

1 _Yes, they did./No, they didn't._

2 _____

3 _____

4 _____

5 _____

30 I feel like dancing!

	verb +	preposition +	-ing		adjective	+ preposition +	-ing
He	talked	**about**	stay**ing** in.	They're	good/bad	**at**	danc**ing**.
I	felt	**like**	watch**ing** TV.	He was	excited	**about**	go**ing** away.
We	succeeded	**in**	find**ing** a house.	She's	interested	**in**	buy**ing** a car.
She's	thinking	**of**	hav**ing** a holiday.	I'm	tired	**of**	work**ing**.
Don't	worry	**about**	gett**ing** a job!	We're	keen	**on**	swimm**ing**.

If a verb comes after a preposition, we usually use the *-ing* form.

A Underline the correct preposition.

ARE YOU A GOOD LANGUAGE LEARNER?

1 Are you good **at/in** learning languages?
2 Do you worry **of/about** getting the pronunciation exactly right?
3 Are you keen **on/about** travelling abroad?
4 Do you always succeed **in/like** passing language exams?
5 Are you interested **in/on** watching foreign language films?
6 Are you thinking **of/by** learning any new languages?

B Complete the sentences with a preposition and the verb in the correct form.

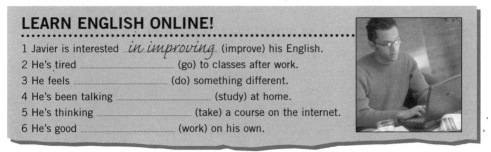

LEARN ENGLISH ONLINE!

1 Javier is interested *in improving* (improve) his English.
2 He's tired .... (go) to classes after work.
3 He feels .... (do) something different.
4 He's been talking .... (study) at home.
5 He's thinking .... (take) a course on the internet.
6 He's good .... (work) on his own.

C Complete the sentences about you. Use a preposition and a verb.

1 I'm good *at* ....
2 I'm not very good ....
3 I'm tired ....
4 I feel ....
5 I'm keen ....
6 I'm interested ....

Test 3 (Units 21–30)

A Circle the correct answer.

1 I'll phone you after I **arrive/'ll arrive**.

2 'What **are/do** your parents like?' 'They're very kind.'

3 I'm **taller/more tall** than my father.

4 'Would you tell me if you **don't like/didn't like** my ideas?' 'Yes, I would.'

5 It's the **fastest/most fast** car I've ever driven.

6 That's the street **who/when/where** I lived.

7 This winter isn't **as colder as/as cold as** last winter.

8 Their pronunciation is difficult **understand/to understand/understanding**.

9 He didn't **used to play/use to play** tennis.

10 I'm thinking **to become/in becoming/of becoming** an actor. | **10** |

B Write the verbs in the present simple or *will* + verb.

1 I (send) _____ you a postcard as soon as I (get) _____ there.

2 When I (see) _____ you, I (show) _____ you the photographs.

3 (you/be) _____ here when I (come) _____ home?

4 What (you/do) _____ after you (have) _____ breakfast?

5 I (always/fall) _____ asleep immediately as soon as I (get) _____ into bed. | **5** |

C Write a comparative or superlative form, or an *as ... as* form.

1 She's _____ teacher in the college. (bad)

2 Is the train station much _____? (far)

3 Your hands are _____ ice. (cold)

4 Italian is much _____ Russian. (easy)

5 What's _____ city you've ever been to? (romantic) | **5** |

D Write the verbs in the correct form.

1 What would she do if she (know) _____ the truth?

2 I (go) _____ and see him more often if he lived nearer.

3 If I (speak) _____ Taiwanese, my job would be a lot easier.

4 I'd marry you if I (have) _____ enough money.

5 If I (not like) _____ your dress, I'd tell you. | **5** |

E Complete the sentences.

1 I know a man _____ has three cars.
2 Is this the train _____ goes to London?
3 That was the year _____ we moved house.
4 The hotel _____ we stayed was very expensive.
5 I know someone _____ lives in that apartment.

[ ] 5

F Write the sentences using the words in brackets.

1 It's _____ early. (important/book)
2 Are you _____ the exam? (worry/do)
3 She's _____ Spanish. (interested/learn)
4 My name is very _____ . (easy/remember)
5 We're _____ the housework. (tired/do)

[ ] 5

G Write sentences with *used to.*

1 men/have/long hair _____
2 I/work/in a factory _____
3 they/not live/in Spain _____
4 where/you/go to college? _____
5 this computer/work _____

[ ] 5

H Correct the mistakes.

1 I'll see you before you <u>will go</u>. _____
2 'What <u>like the weather</u>?' 'It was great.' _____
3 '<u>How were your teachers at school?</u>' 'They were nice.' _____
4 She's got more money <u>that</u> I have. _____
5 These days your brother is much <u>friendlyer</u>. _____
6 If I <u>feel</u> ill, I would go to a doctor. _____
7 It's <u>most famous</u> theatre in St Petersburg. _____
8 Who was the woman <u>which</u> was wearing jeans? _____
9 I <u>used to</u> go out last night at 10.00 pm. _____
10 He succeeded <u>to pass</u> his exams. _____

[ ] 10

TOTAL [ ] 50

31 She speaks clearly

Regular adverbs		Irregular adverbs	
Adjectives	Adverbs	Adjectives	Adverbs
perfect	perfectly	good	well
horrible	horribly	late/hard	late/hard

Adjectives usually come before the noun or after verbs like *be* and *look*.
Adverbs often come after the verb (She sings **well**.) or after the object (He speaks English **well**. NOT He speaks well English.). They do not come between the verb and the object.

ⓘ Some *-ly* adjectives: *early, friendly, lively, lovely, silly* have no adverbs.

A Underline the correct word.

Fausto: You look (1) **tired/tiredly**. Did you go to bed (2) **late/lately** last night?

Sandra: No, I didn't, but I slept (3) **bad/badly**.

Fausto: Were you (4) **worried/worriedly** about the meeting today?

Sandra: No, there was a band in the street all night. They played (5) **beautiful/beautifully** but they were very (6) **loud/loudly** and I couldn't sleep.

B Make the adjectives into adverbs. Write them in the correct places.

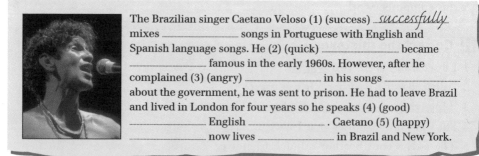

The Brazilian singer Caetano Veloso (1) (success) *successfully* mixes .... songs in Portuguese with English and Spanish language songs. He (2) (quick) .... became .... famous in the early 1960s. However, after he complained (3) (angry) .... in his songs .... about the government, he was sent to prison. He had to leave Brazil and lived in London for four years so he speaks (4) (good) .... English .... Caetano (5) (happy) .... now lives .... in Brazil and New York.

C Choose an adverb from the box and write sentences about you.

badly   beautifully   carefully   hard   quickly   slowly   ~~well~~

1 *I don't sing very well.* .... (sing)
2 .... (study)
3 .... (walk)
4 .... (read English)
5 .... (drive)

32 It's hot, isn't it?

Positive sentence + negative tag
It's hot, **isn't** it? They **finished** their lunch, **didn't** they? They**'ve** eaten, **haven't** they?

Negative sentence + positive tag
Tom **doesn't smoke, does** he? She**'s** not **going** to be late, **is** she? I **can't** go, **can** I?
We use the correct form of *be*, *have*, *do* or a modal in the question tag.
ⓘ We use question tags when we think the other person agrees with us, or when we want the other person to agree with us.
! I**'m** late, **aren't** I? (NOT ~~am I not?~~)

A Match the two parts of the sentence.

1 You don't like programmes about politics, ___*e*___   **a** didn't we?

2 'The Fast Show' was funny last week, ___   **b** have we?

3 We saw that film last month, ___   **c** can't you?

4 Anthony Hopkins is a very good actor, ___   **d** won't it?

5 The programme will be on TV again next week, ___   **e** do you?

6 We haven't seen this programme before, ___   **f** wasn't it

7 You can get a better picture than that, ___   **g** isn't he?

B Write question tags for this interview with a TV producer.

1 (You made the film 'The Life of Animals', *didn't you?*)

2 (You don't make many programmes about animals, ___)

3 (Programmes about animals are difficult to make, ___)

4 (Your next film is about modern art, ___)

5 (You're going to make it in France, ___)

6 (You haven't started it yet, ___)

7 (It won't cost a lot of money, ___)

8 (I'm right, ___)

33 There's no-one at home

	some	*any*	*no*
People	someone/somebody	anyone/anybody	no-one/nobody
Things	something	anything	nothing
Place	somewhere	anywhere	nowhere
Positive	I've lost **something**. There is **no-one** here. (NOT ~~There isn't no-one here.~~)		
Negative	I can't find him **anywhere**. There isn't **anyone** here.		
Questions	Is there **anyone** here?		

ⓘ Do you want **anything**? (Question) Would you like **something** to eat? (We expect the answer 'yes' – for example, in offers and requests.)

A Underline the correct answer.

1 There isn't **anything/something** on the desk.

2 **Someone/No-one** is on the phone.

3 There's **somewhere/nowhere** to stay.

4 There's **nothing/something** to eat.

5 I can't see **anything/anyone**.

6 Do you need **anything/nothing**?

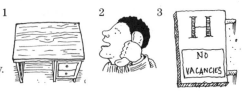

B These people are at a conference. Complete the sentences with a *some-*, *any-* or *no-* word.

1 Does ___*anyone*___ have any questions?

2 Here's _____ to read before the next talk.

3 I've met you _____ before, but I can't remember where.

4 Do you know _____ about the next speaker?

5 I'm looking for _____, but I can't find her _____ .

6 Sorry, there's _____ to sit. Can you get a chair from another room?

7 I'm going for a walk. There's _____ interesting on the programme at the moment.

8 Does _____ have _____ to say? No? Then let's finish!

34 It was too cold to go out

too + adjective/adverb (*too* = more than is good)
We didn't play tennis yesterday. It was (much) **too** hot. We didn't reach the top of the mountain. We climbed (much) **too** slowly.
not + adjective/adverb + enough (*not enough* = less than is good)
I couldn't hear the music. It was**n't** loud **enough**. She lost the race. She did**n't** run quickly **enough** in the last 200 metres.
After *too* and *not … enough* we can use the *to*-infinitive or *for* + noun/pronoun. He's **too** young **to go** to work. He's **not** old **enough for** the job.
ⓘ *too* is different from *very*. It's **very** cold. (but maybe it's OK.) It's **too** cold. Let's stay at home! (It's not OK.) It was a **very** hot day. (*very* + adj + noun) NOT ~~It was a too hot day.~~

A Write sentences saying why the car is not right. Use *too* or *not … enough*.

WANTED
Large car (for 3 children!)
Very big boot
Age: about 4 years old
Quiet engine
About £5000

1 (the car/quiet) *The car isn't quiet enough.*

2 (the boot/small) *The boot is too small.*

3 (the car/big) .

4 (the car/noisy)

5 (it/cheap)

6 (it/old)

B Join these sentences using *too* or *not … enough*.

1 The mirror was heavy. I didn't carry it home.
   The mirror was too heavy to carry home.

2 Pippa isn't very strong. She can't lift the suitcase.
   Pippa isn't strong enough to lift the suitcase.

3 The suit was formal. I couldn't wear it to the party.

4 I don't feel very well. I don't want to eat.

5 Olga was tired. She didn't go shopping.

6 Your car isn't very safe. I don't want to drive it.

35 They are made in Taiwan

The passive   ⏩ Irregular verbs page 61

Positive		Negative		
The cars **were** **made** in Japan.		Tea	**isn't**	**grown** in England.
Question				
Are the windows **broken?**		How many	windows	**were** **broken?**

We form the passive with the correct form of *be* + past participle. We use the passive when we do not know, or it is not important, who does something.

ⓘ When we want to say who/what did the action we use *by*. Tara **was met by** her brother.

A Underline the correct answer.

1 These leather bags **make/<u>are made</u>** in Portugal.

2 We **buy/are bought** these rugs in Turkey.

3 These clothes **wear/are worn** by some people in Mexico.

4 Where **are/do** those musical instruments **came/come** from?

5 This jewellery **comes/is come** from India.

6 Who **paints/is painted** those wooden toys?

7 They **sell/are sold** these hats in Russia.

8 These masks **bring/are brought** from Africa.

B Write the verb in the present simple passive.

Our market (1) ....*is divided*........ (divide) into two parts: clothes .... (sell) outdoors and food (3) .... (sell) indoors. Everything (4) .... (bring) to the market early in the morning. The clothes (5) .... (take) out of the van and we check that they (6) .... (price) correctly. At the end of the day the goods (7) .... (put away) in the van. Then, after we leave, there's a lot of mess, which (8) .... (clean up) by a large group of cleaners.

C Match the verbs with the past participles in the box.

| arrested | killed | ~~robbed~~ | stolen | injured | broken into |

1 rob _robbed_

2 break into _____

3 steal _____

4 arrest _____

5 injure _____

6 kill _____

D Complete this news story with 5 verbs from Exercise C in the past simple passive.

DIFFICULT YEAR FOR LONDON

According to a recent report, last year 63,000 cars (1) _were stolen_ in the capital, 36,000 people (2) _____ in the street, and 129,000 houses and offices (3) _____ . On the roads, things were not much better. 300 people (4) _____ in serious accidents and, 4,600 (5) _____ and went to hospital.

E Now complete these questions and answers.

1 How many _cars were stolen_ _____ ? 63,000
2 How many _____ ? 36,000
3 How many _____ ? 129,000
4 _____ over 200 people _____ in serious accidents? _____ they _____ .
5 How many _____ in road accidents? 4,600

F Complete the conversation. Use the past simple passive.

1 **A**: my car/steal/last month _My car was stolen last month._
2 **B**: the car/find? _____
3 **A**: Yes, it/find/in a field _____
4 **B**: the thief/catch? _____
5 **A**: Yes, he/arrest/by the police _____
6 **B**: he/send/to prison? _____
7 **A**: No, he/not./He/fine/a lot of money _____

36 There are too many people

too much + uncountable nouns	too many + countable nouns
I bought too much milk.	She reads too many books.
not ... enough + countable and uncountable nouns	
She doesn't drink enough water.	They didn't bring enough cakes.

A Write *too much, too many* or *not enough* in the gaps.

1 *too many* books
2 *not enough* water
3 .... bread
4 .... coffee
5 .... apples
6 .... money

B Complete the doctor's advice with *too much, too many* or *not enough.*

Health Questionnaire

How many hours do you work?	60 per week
How much sleep do you get?	10 hours a night
How much exercise do you get?	1 short walk a week
What do you usually eat?	Beef, potatoes, chocolate cake and lots of sweet drinks

1 You work *too many* hours a week.
2 You spend .... time asleep.
3 You (do) .... exercise.
4 You eat .... meat and .... potatoes.
5 There (be) .... green vegetables in your diet.
6 There's .... sugar in your diet.
7 You drink .... sweet drinks.

C Write about you using *too much, too many* or *not enough.*

1 I (work) *I work too many hours./I don't work enough hours.*
2 I (do exercise) ....
3 I (eat) ....
4 There (be) .... in my diet.
5 I (drink) ....

37 I've been working here for 6 months

Present perfect continuous (positive)

I've We've (have) You've They've	been	watching TV.	He's She's (has) It's	been	waiting.
She's (has)	been	learning French	for six months. since 2001.		

We use the present perfect continuous for actions that started in the past and are continuing now or have only recently stopped.

A Look at the pictures. What have the people been doing? Use verbs from the box and the present perfect continuous.

cook   paint   play   shop   walk

1 *They've been playing tennis.*

2 ....

3 ....

4 ....

5 ....

B Write *for* or *since* in the gaps.

1 *for* two weeks 2 .... yesterday 3 .... 8.30 am

4 .... a few days 5 .... your birthday 6 .... a year

7 .... last year 8 .... Monday 9 .... we met

C Write sentences about you with *since* and *for* and the present perfect continuous.

1 (I/work) *I've been working in my company for 3 years. (OR since 2001)*

2 (I/live) ....

3 (I/learn) ....

4 (I/sit) ....

5 (I/wear) ....

38 I would like you to come

	verb	+ object/person	+ to-infinitive
I	**want** **would like** **need**	her/you	**to** leave.
Question:		Do you **want/need** me to ...? **Would** you **like** me **to** ...?	
She	**told** **asked**	him/her	(not) **to** hurry.

Other verbs: *advise, encourage, expect, persuade, remind*

A A manager is talking to an assistant. Complete with *want, would like* or *need*.

ACTION POINTS
* Check sales figures
* Send fax
* Order more paper
* Book meeting room
* Do filing
* Arrange trip to Boston
* Photocopy report

1 I *want/would like/need you to check* the sales figures.

2 Do you *want/need me to send* the fax?

3 I _____ more paper.

4 I _____ a meeting room.

5 Would you _____ the filing?

6 Do you _____ the trip to Boston?

7 I _____ the report.

B Read the notes and complete the sentences.

How green is your office?
● think about the office environment
● recycle more
● cycle to work
● use less paper
● turn off the lights at night
● shut down computers

1 They *asked us to think* _____ about our office environment. (ask)

2 They _____ more. (tell)

3 They _____ to work. (encourage)

4 They _____ less paper. (persuade)

5 They _____ the lights at night. (remind)

6 They _____ our computers when we weren't using them. (advise)

39 I sent her a card

Pattern 1			Pattern 2			
verb	+ object 2	+ object 1	verb	+ object 1	+ *to/for*	+ object 2
I lent	my brother	some money.	I lent	some money	to	my brother.
He bought	his friend	a car.	He bought	a car	for	his friend.

Verbs + *to*: *give, lend, offer, pass, pay, read, send, show, teach*

Verbs + *for*: *bring, buy, find, get, make, cook, order*

ⓘ Pattern 1 is more common when object 2 is a personal pronoun: I took him a present. (BUT I took it to him. NOT ~~I took him it.~~)

Quickjet Airlines

A Underline the correct answer.

1 <u>They offered us more choice</u>./They more choice offered us.
2 They sent us the tickets by email./They sent to us the tickets by email.
3 They lent to us a car./They lent us a car.
4 The steward our seats showed us./The steward showed us our seats.
5 He found us good seats at the front./He found good seats us at the front.
6 A vegetarian meal I ordered my friend./I ordered a vegetarian meal for my friend.

B Write *to* or *for* in the gaps. Then write the sentence as Pattern 1.

1 I'll find a place _*for*_ you to sit. *I'll find you a place to sit.*
2 We'll get a sandwich _____ you later. _____
3 Will you give the blanket _____ me? _____
4 Pass that book _____ me, will you? _____
5 Get some earphones _____ me, too. _____
6 Shall I read the menu _____ you? _____

C Write sentences using Pattern 1 or Pattern 2.

1 (1 you/a free meal) They offer _*you a free meal*_ if the flight is delayed.
2 (2 their customers/excellent service) They give _____
3 (1 you/great films) They show _____
4 (2 their customers/good hotels) They find _____
5 (2 cheap tickets/anyone) They sell _____ who books early.
6 (1 people/the truth) They always tell _____ in advertisements!

40 It was sunny but very cold

and
I got dressed **and** (I) had my breakfast.
I got up, got dressed, had some breakfast **and** (then) went to work.

but
Sue hasn't got a car **but** her brother has (got a car).

because (= reason)
I went to the bank **because** I needed some money.

so (= result)
I needed some money **so** I went to the bank.

ⓘ With *and* sentences it is not necessary to repeat the subject.

A Write the correct word in the gaps.

1 St Petersburg is one of the greatest ......*and*...... most beautiful cities in the world. (and/but/so)

2 We plan your visit carefully .... we want you to enjoy your stay. (but/because/so)

3 You have only 3 days there .... you'll be very busy. (because/so)

4 It's very cold in winter .... in summer the temperature goes up to 30°C. (because/so/but)

5 In June the days are very long .... the nights are very short. (because/and/but)

6 There are many beautiful sights .... bring your camera! (because/so/but)

B Join each pair of sentences with *and, but, so, because.*

1 *Peter the Great built a castle because he wanted to protect the Neva River.*

2 ....

3 ....

4 ....

5 ....

HISTORY OF ST PETERSBURG
(1) Peter the Great built a castle. He wanted to protect the Neva River. (2) Peter loved European architecture. He invited an Italian architect to design a new capital. (3) The city was difficult to build. The land was very wet and soft. (4) The work was very dangerous. Over 100,000 workers lost their lives. (5) In 1712 the city became the capital of Russia. In 1918 the capital changed back to Moscow.

Test 4 (Units 31–40)

A Circle the correct answer.

1 She ran away **quick/quickly**.
2 You can't swim, **can't you?/can you?**
3 I can't hear **anyone/no-one**.
4 The car wasn't in **very/too** good condition.
5 This television **made/was made** in Japan.
6 He's got **too many/too much** work.
7 I've been studying English **for/since** I was a child.
8 We'd like you **sit/to sit** down.
9 She gave **me/to me** the money.
10 It was very cold **so/because** we didn't go out.

10

B Make the adjective into an adverb and write it in the correct position in the sentence.

1 He read the letter. (slow) ⎯⎯⎯⎯⎯⎯⎯⎯⎯⎯⎯⎯⎯⎯⎯
2 She tried to remember his name. (hard) ⎯⎯⎯⎯⎯⎯⎯⎯⎯
3 It rained. (heavy) ⎯⎯⎯⎯⎯⎯⎯⎯⎯⎯⎯⎯⎯⎯⎯⎯⎯⎯⎯
4 I understand you. (perfect) ⎯⎯⎯⎯⎯⎯⎯⎯⎯⎯⎯⎯⎯⎯
5 He went to bed. (late) ⎯⎯⎯⎯⎯⎯⎯⎯⎯⎯⎯⎯⎯⎯⎯⎯⎯

5

C Write the question tag.

1 She didn't go last week, ⎯⎯⎯⎯⎯⎯⎯⎯⎯ ?
2 You like this music, ⎯⎯⎯⎯⎯⎯⎯ ?
3 That bag was very expensive, ⎯⎯⎯⎯⎯⎯⎯ ?
4 I'm coming with you, ⎯⎯⎯⎯⎯⎯⎯ ?
5 You haven't seen this film before, ⎯⎯⎯⎯⎯⎯⎯ ?

5

D Complete the words with *some-*, *any-* or *no-*.

1 I found ⎯⎯⎯⎯⎯thing interesting on his desk. Come and have a look!
2 She doesn't have ⎯⎯⎯⎯⎯where to live.
3 ⎯⎯⎯⎯⎯thing ever happens in this town. It's boring!
4 He went to the meeting but there wasn't ⎯⎯⎯⎯⎯one there.
5 Haven't I seen you ⎯⎯⎯⎯⎯where before?

5

E Change two sentences into one. Use the word(s) in brackets.

1 This soup is very hot. I can't eat it. (too) ....

2 You can't drive. You're too young. (not ... enough) ....

3 She's very excited. She can't sleep. (too) ....

4 I'm not very well. I can't go out. (not ... enough) ....

5 He's very old. He can't work. (too) **5**

F Write the verb in the correct form.

1 This house (paint) .... last month.

2 Millions of people (read) .... this newspaper every day.

3 My wallet (steal) .... last night.

4 Indian languages (still/speak) .... in parts of Mexico.

5 (*Romeo and Juliet*/write) .... by Shakespeare? **5**

G Write sentences in the present perfect continuous.

1 I/play/tennis ....

2 She/study/six years ....

3 He/work/here/he was sixteen ....

4 They/live/in Scotland/ten weeks ....

5 We/write/postcards/10 o'clock **5**

H Write the words in the correct order to make a sentence.

1 you not go advise I to ....

2 some can lend me you money ....

3 mother bought present she for a her ....

4 me flowers buy he to told some ....

5 dinner a cooked her lovely I **5**

I Correct the mistakes.

1 It's not <u>enough warm</u> to go swimming. ....

2 He's got <u>too many</u> money. ....

3 We'd like <u>that you sit down</u>. ....

4 I sent <u>to her</u> a CD. ....

5 <u>Because it was late, so we went home.</u> **5**

TOTAL **50**

Irregular verbs

VERB	PAST SIMPLE	PAST PARTICIPLE
be	was/were	been
become	became	become
begin	began	begun
break	broke	broken
bring	brought	brought
buy	bought	bought
catch	caught	caught
come	came	come
do	did	done
drink	drank	drunk
drive	drove	driven
eat	ate	eaten
feel	felt	felt
find	found	found
get	got	got
give	gave	given
go	went	gone/been
grow	grew	grown
have	had	had
hurt	hurt	hurt
know	knew	known
learn	learned/learnt	learned/learnt
leave	left	left
lie	lay	lain
lend	lent	lent
lose	lost	lost
make	made	made
meet	met	met
pay	paid	paid
put	put	put
read	read	read
run	ran	run
say	said	said

VERB	PAST SIMPLE	PAST PARTICIPLE
see	saw	seen
sell	sold	sold
send	sent	sent
set up	set up	set up
shine	shone	shone
sing	sang	sung
sit	sat	sat
sleep	slept	slept
speak	spoke	spoken
spend	spent	spent
steal	stole	stolen
swim	swam	swum
take	took	taken
teach	taught	taught
tell	told	told
think	thought	thought
understand	understood	understood
wake	woke	woken
wear	wore	worn
win	won	won
write	wrote	written

Answer key

Unit 1

A 2 Is your job difficult?
3 Are you happy at work?
4 Have you got a lot of friends at work?
5 Are your colleagues helpful?
6 Is your manager pleased with your work?
7 Have you got a company car?
8 Has your company got a gym?

B 2 Yes, it is. / No, it isn't.
3 Yes, I am. / No, I'm not.
4 Yes I have. / No, I haven't.
5 Yes, they are. / No, they're not. / No, they aren't.
6 Yes, he/she is. / No, he/she isn't.
7 Yes, I have. / No, I haven't.
8 Yes, it has. / No, it hasn't.

Unit 2

A 2 had 3 doesn't have/hasn't got
4 has/has got 5 has 6 have

B 2 has / doesn't have / 's got / hasn't got a lot of expensive shops
3 've got / haven't got / have / don't have …(Answers will vary.)
4 had / didn't have a big population
5 had / didn't have… (Answers will vary.)
6 had / didn't have… (Answers will vary.)

Unit 3

A 2 is talking 3 are standing 4 is holding
5 are ('re) wearing 6 isn't smiling

B 2 is she holding 3 Are they talking
4 is the mother looking
5 Is the sun shining

C 2 are sleeping 3 is watching
4 are working 5 is doing

D 2 are working more/less.
3 are staying single/getting married.
4 are getting bigger/getting smaller.
5 are leaving home earlier/leaving home later.

Unit 4

A 2 has 3 don't understand 4 speak 5 play
6 wear 7 eat

B 2 do the world's fastest land animals live? B
3 do 90% of families own A
4 does the New Year last; take place F
5 do restaurants serve D
6 do people eat E

C 2 sells property and writes comic books
3 live in Britain and are interested in politics
4 owns supermarkets and drives old cars
5 sell newspapers and collect art
6 comes from Dubai and likes horseracing

D 2 doesn't. She lives in Hong Kong.
3 don't. They make their money from motor racing.
4 doesn't. He comes from America.
5 don't. They love art.
6 doesn't. He works in the oil business.

Unit 5

A 2 She goes to the doctor about three times a year.
3 She sometimes has a headache in the evenings.
4 She rarely feels depressed.
5 She hardly ever stays off work.
6 She gets some exercise every day.

B Answers will vary.

Unit 6

A 2 's working 3 likes 4 never gets
5 doesn't travel 6 's making

B 2 Are you working for UNICEF in India? Yes I am.
3 Do you like trips like this? Yes, I do.
4 Do you (ever) get much sleep? No, I don't.
5 Does Tim travel with you? No, he doesn't.
6 Is he making a film? Yes, he is.

C 2 's acting 3 likes 4 's not dancing
5 lives 6 are watching

D 2 Are you watching TV at the moment?
3 Do you sometimes listen to music at
work?
4 Does/do your family live with you?
5 Where are you doing this exercise?
6 What do you want to do later today?

E Answers will vary.

Unit 7

A 2 used 3 set up 4 became 5 sold
6 introduced 7 started

B 2 opened 3 made 4 created 5 were
6 went 7 didn't sell 8 did 9 won

C 2 Did they offer 3 Did you say
4 Was the job 5 Were you happy
6 Did you stay
MASASHI 2 Yes, they did.
3 No, I didn't. 4 No, it wasn't.
5 Yes, I was. 6 No, I didn't
YOU Answers will vary.

D Answers will vary. (Past tenses: arrived,
got, used, wrote, had, shouted, went,
made, enjoyed, left)

Unit 8

A 2 What (Which) currency do people use?
3 How many people live
4 Which army attacked
5 What does Mexico export?
6 What (Which) language do most people speak?
7 Who lives in the National Palace?

B 2 How many people travelled
3 Who paid 4 Who met you
5 Which hotel did you stay at?
6 How many other companies did you
visit?
7 Who paid

Unit 9

A 2 was hitting 3 wasn't enjoying
4 was teaching 5 were dancing
6 was wishing

B 2 were flying 3 was standing
4 was wearing 5 was holding

6 was singing 7 weren't looking
8 were watching 9 were walking
10 was shining 11 were singing
12 were running 13 was running

Unit 10

A 2 it raining (hard)?
3 wheel come off?
4 you decide to do
5 did you realise
6 were you doing

B 2 Yes, it was.
3 were driving into the city centre.
4 (We decided) to walk.
5 were checking into our hotel.
6 was telephoning the airport.

C 2 was singing, lost
3 dropped, were carrying
4 saw, was sitting
5 stopped, wasn't wearing
6 were lying, didn't know
7 were running, started

D 2 Were you singing
3 Where were you taking 4 Did he see
5 What were they saying
6 Were other people lying
7 Why were they running

E Answers will vary.

Test 1 (Units 1–10)

A 1 got a new manager 2 had 3 is the man
4 believe 5 never takes 6 'm writing
7 get 8 lives 9 were you lying
10 were playing

B 1 were 2 's got/has 3 Did, have
4 Has, got / Does, have 5 Are, 'm

C 1 's getting 2 Do you understand, don't
3 does he come, think 4 are sitting
5 are they staying, Do you know

D 1 We hardly ever finish 2 she ever eat
3 tired every evening. 4 Was he always
5 They rarely went

E 1 Were you standing, happened
2 visiting, introduced 3 met, were
travelling 4 didn't like, was 5 was having,
woke

F 1 Who wrote 2 Where did you buy

3 Who's cooking 4 Which team won
5 How many people live
6 What did she eat 7 Who ate
8 What happened
9 What are they studying
10 Which train goes

G 1 your job difficult 2 didn't have
3 didn't 4 living 5 sells 6 like
7 usually live 8 didn't know 9 said
10 was already shining

Unit 11

A 2 a 3 the 4 the 5 a 6 the 7 the, the
8 The

B 2 the 3 the 4 a 5 the 6 the 7 The 8 the
9 a 10 The 11 The 12 the

Unit 12

A 2 I'm meeting 3 will you 4 He'll tell
5 Shall I 6 Danuta's going to 7 won't
listen

B 2 'll get 3 'll be 4 're not doing
5 'll have 6 're staying 7 're meeting
8 won't be 9 'll take 10 Shall I book

C 2 you won't be (Sweden) 3 Shall I book
(Egypt) 4 I'm going (Hawaii) 5 are you
going to eat (Japan) 6 I'll take (India)

Unit 13

A 2 don't have to pay 3 don't have to buy
4 have to take 5 have to book

B 2 Did Nadia have to wear, did
3 Will Rob have to play, won't
4 Will Lois have to have, won't
5 Did you have to buy, didn't
6 do I have to book

Unit 14

A 3 Kyoto University
4 Kyoto 5 the 19th century 6 on foot
7 temples 8 lovely gardens 9 Japanese
10 The Japanese 11 English

B 1) 2 X 3 X 4 X 5 X
2) 1 X 2 the 3 X 4 X 5 the 6 X 7 the 8 X
3) 1 X 2 the 3 the 4 X 5 the

Unit 15

A 2 D, mustn't 3 A, shouldn't 4 C, must
5 B, should 6 E, shouldn't

B 2 should 3 must 4 mustn't 5 must
6 mustn't

Unit 16

A 2 a couple of 3 some 4 a lot of 5 several
6 plenty of

B 2 There are a couple of security cameras.
3 There is some expensive furniture.
4 There are a lot of shelves.
5 There isn't any fax paper.
6 There are a few filing cabinets.

C 2 many 3 any 4 a few 5 a lot of
6 Many 7 a little 8 much 9 a couple of
10 many 11 a lot of 12 a lot of

D 2 many; Not many./Not too many.
3 many; A few. /Not a lot.
4 much; Not much./Not too much.
5 many; A couple.

E Answers will vary.

Unit 17

A 2 have crossed 3 has just broken
4 has already run 5 has never won
6 have just agreed

B 2 broken, have, broke
3 made, haven't, have been
4 been, have, was
5 lost, haven't, have always made

C Answers will vary.

D 2 married 3 have been 4 has appeared
5 played 6 started 7 has always been
8 decided 9 has also had
10 hasn't always been 11 hated 12 were

Unit 18

A 2 serving 3 to arrive 4 to buy
5 booking 6 wearing

B 2 to go 3 eating 4 to sit 5 raining
6 to tell 7 to get 8 to hear 9 feeling

C Answers will vary.

Unit 19

A 2 c 3 a 4 d 5 f 6 e

B Answers will vary.

C 2 arrive, 'll put 3 want, 'll find
4 get, relax 5 need, 'll see
6 arrive, don't forget

Unit 20

A Answers will vary.

B 2 couldn't 3 can't 4 couldn't 5 can

Test 2 (Units 11–20)

A 1 the 2 Shall I 3 Do you have to drive
4 good Russian 5 should 6 a little
7 stayed 8 smoking 9 gets 10 couldn't

B 1 the 2 a 3 the 4 X, X 5 X

C 1 snows, 'll go 2 've known 3 Shall
4 see, 'll ask 5 've lost

D 1 're going ('re going to go)
2 Did you have 3 Will 4 'll 5 don't

E 1 Did you have to 2 had to
3 won't have to 4 didn't have to
5 will you have to

F 1 must 2 shouldn't 3 mustn't 4 should
5 mustn't

G 1 much 2 several 3 many, A few
4 a lot of 5 any

H 1 to tell 2 to send 3 laughing 4 getting
5 to help

I 1 couldn't 2 can't 3 could 4 can't 5 can

Unit 21

A 2 finds 3 gets 4 likes 5 arrives 6 returns
7 gets up 8 phones 9 has 10 gets on
11 goes

B 2 will meet, arrive 3 finish 4 get back
5 finish, 'll arrange 6 lands

Unit 22

A 2 d 3 a 4 e 5 b

B 2 What's the money like?
3 What were the other people like?
4 What's the job like?
5 What was the office like?
6 What were the computers like?

C 2 What was the food like?
3 What were the the people like?
4 What was the flight like?
5 What were the beaches like?

Unit 23

A 3 The Crown is smaller than The Star.
4 The Star has (got) a lot more facilities
than The Crown.
5 The Star is more modern than The
Crown.
6 The Star is more expensive than The
Crown.
7 The Crown is cheaper than The Star.
8 The Star is better than The Crown.

B 2 more interesting 3 more comfortable
4 brighter 5 newer 6 dirtier 7 better
8 nearer 9 noisier 10 more attractive

Unit 24

A 2 didn't like 3 would 4 gave 5 would

B 2 found, would you read
3 Would you say, forgot
4 took, would you return
5 Would you leave, hit
6 was, would you tell

C 2 I would/wouldn't read
3 I would/wouldn't say
4 I would/wouldn't return
5 I would/wouldn't leave
6 I would/wouldn't tell

Unit 25

A 2 the lowest 3 the fastest 4 the best
5 the highest 6 the most interesting
7 the worst

B 1 best, most famous
2 finest, highest, cheapest, busiest
3 most romantic, most popular

Unit 26

A 2 who 3 when 4 that 5 which 6 where

B Answers will vary. 2 who/that are …
3 when … 4 that/which …
5 that/which … 6 where …

C 2 He wears jeans that/which don't fit.
3 She has a brother who/that sends them money.
4 They have a dog that/which hates loud noises.
5 They love weekends when they can be together.

Unit 27

A 2 isn't as small as 3 isn't as wet as
4 is almost as hot as 5 isn't quite as hot as
6 isn't as dry as 7 isn't as large as

B Answers will vary.
2 is/isn't as healthy as
3 is/isn't as dangerous as
4 are/aren't as horrible as
5 are/aren't as intelligent as
6 was/wasn't as important as
7 is/isn't as interesting as

Unit 28

A 2 to win (to get) 3 to understand
4 to walk 5 to get

B 2 best to stay 3 happy to do
4 lucky to get 5 right to buy
6 good to see

C Answers will vary.
2 ... difficult to learn.
3 ... easy to understand.
4 ... impossible to remember.
5 ... nice to eat.

Unit 29

A 2 C, used to act 3 D, used to play
4 E, used to teach 5 B, used to work
6 F, used to be

B 2 Did women use to stay at home more?
3 Did children use to read more?
4 Did you use to listen to the radio a lot?
5 Did men and women use to get married earlier?

C 2, 3 and 5 Yes, they did./No, they didn't.
4 Yes, I did./No, I didn't.

Unit 30

A 2 about 3 on 4 in 5 in 6 of

B 2 of going 3 like doing 4 about studying
5 of taking 6 at working

C Answers will vary. All verbs + -ing.
1 good at (swimming) ...
2 not very good at ... 3 tired of ...
4 feel like ... 5 keen on ...
6 interested in

Test 3 (Units 21–30)

A 1 arrive 2 are 3 taller 4 didn't like
5 fastest 6 where 7 as cold as
8 to understand 9 use to play
10 of becoming

B 1 'll send, get 2 see, 'll show
3 Will you be, come 4 will you do/do you do, have 5 always fall, get

C 1 the worst 2 further (farther)
3 as cold as (colder than) 4 easier than
5 the most romantic

D 1 knew 2 would go 3 spoke 4 had
5 didn't like

E 1 who (that) 2 that (which)
3 when (that) 4 where 5 who (that)

F 1 important to book
2 worried about doing
3 interested in learning
4 easy to remember 5 tired of doing

G 1 Men used to have long hair.
2 I used to work in a factory.
3 They didn't use to live in Spain.
4 Where did you use to go to college?
5 This computer used to work.

H 1 go 2 was the weather like
3 What were your teachers at school like?
4 than 5 friendlier 6 felt
7 the most famous 8 who (that) 9 went
10 in passing

Unit 31

A 2 late 3 badly 4 worried 5 beautifully
6 loud

B 2 ... quickly became
3 ... complained angrily
4 ... English well 5 ... lives happily

C Answers will vary.

Unit 32

A 2 f 3 a 4 g 5 d 6 b 7 c

B 2 do you? 3 aren't they? 4 isn't it?
5 aren't you? 6 have you? 7 will it?
8 aren't I?

Unit 33

A 2 Someone 3 nowhere 4 nothing
5 anything 6 anything

B 2 something 3 somewhere 4 anything
5 someone/somebody, anywhere
6 nowhere 7 nothing 8 anyone, anything

Unit 34

A 3 The car isn't big enough.
4 The car is too noisy.
5 It isn't cheap enough. 6 It's too old.

B 3 The suit was too formal to wear to the
party./... too formal for the party.
4 I don't feel well enough to eat.
5 Olga was too tired to go shopping./
... too tired for shopping.
6 Your car isn't safe enough to drive.

Unit 35

A 2 buy 3 are worn 4 do, come 5 comes
6 paints 7 sell 8 are brought

B 2 are sold 3 is sold 4 is brought
5 are taken 6 are priced 7 are put away
8 is cleaned up

C 2 broken into 3 stolen 4 arrested
5 injured 6 killed

D 2 were robbed 3 were broken into
4 were killed 5 were injured

E 2 people were robbed
3 houses and offices were broken into
4 Were, killed, Yes, were 5 people were
injured

F 2 Was the car found?
3 Yes, it was found in a field.
4 Was the thief caught?
5 Yes, he was arrested by the police.
6 Was he sent to prison?
7 No, he wasn't. He was fined a lot of
money.

Unit 36

A 3 too much 4 too much
5 too many 6 not enough

B 2 too much 3 don't do enough
4 too much, too many 5 aren't enough
6 too much 7 too many

C Answers will vary.

Unit 37

A 2 They've been walking.
3 She's been painting.
4 He's been shopping.
5 He's been cooking.

B 2 since 3 since 4 for 5 since 6 for
7 since 8 since 9 since

C Answers will vary.
2 I've been living ...
3 I've been learning ...
4 I've been sitting ...
5 I've been wearing ...

Unit 38

A 3 want/need/would like you to order
4 want/need/would like you to book
5 like me to do
6 want/need me to arrange
7 want/need/would like you to photocopy

B 2 told us to recycle
3 encouraged us to cycle
4 persuaded us to use
5 reminded us to turn off
6 advised us to shut down our

Unit 39

A 2 They sent us the tickets by email.
3 They lent us a car.
4 The steward showed us our seats.
5 He found us good seats at the front.
6 I ordered a vegetarian meal for my
friend.

B 2 for, We'll get you a sandwich later.
3 to, Will you give me the blanket?
4 to, Pass me that book, will you?
5 for, Get me some earphones too.
6 to, Shall I read you the menu?

C 2 excellent service to their customers.
3 you great films.
4 good hotels for their customers.
5 cheap tickets to anyone
6 people the truth

Unit 40

A 2 because 3 so 4 but 5 and 6 so

B 2 Peter loved European architecture so he invited an Italian architect to design a new capital.
3 The city was difficult to build because the land was very wet and soft.
4 The work was very dangerous and over 100,000 workers lost their lives.
5 In 1712 the city became the capital of Russia but in 1918 the capital changed back to Moscow.

Test 4 (Units 31–40)

A 1 quickly 2 can you? 3 anyone 4 very
5 was made 6 too much 7 since 8 to sit
9 me 10 so

B 1 He read the letter slowly.
2 She tried hard to remember his name.
3 It rained heavily.
4 I understand you perfectly.
5 He went to bed late.

C 1 did she 2 don't you 3 wasn't it
4 aren't I 5 have you

D 1 some 2 any 3 No 4 any 5 some

E 1 This soup is too hot to eat.
2 You're not old enough to drive.
3 She's too excited to sleep.
4 I'm not well enough to go out.
5 He's too old to work.

F 1 was painted 2 read 3 was stolen
4 are still spoken
5 Was *Romeo and Juliet* written

G 1 I've been playing tennis.
2 She's been studying for six years.
3 He's been working here since he was sixteen.
4 They've been living in Scotland for ten weeks.
5 We've been writing postcards since 10 o'clock.

H 1 I advise you not to go.
2 Can you lend me some money?
3 She bought a present for her mother.
4 He told me to buy some flowers.
5 I cooked her a lovely dinner.

I 1 warm enough 2 too much
3 you to sit down 4 her
5 It was late, so we went home. /
Because it was late, we went home.

Acknowledgements

I would particularly like to thank Alison Sharpe for her help, guidance and support during the editing of this series. My thanks to Pat Chappell and Jamie Smith for their expert editing of the material and to Kamae Design and Nick Schon for their excellent design and artwork.

The publisher would like to thank the following for permission to reproduce photographs.
p. 38 arcblue.com/Peter Durant (modern hotel); p. 6 The Bridgeman Art Library (Courtyard of a House in Delft, 1658 (oil on Canvas), Hooch, Pieter de, 1629-84); p. 8 Corbis/D. Lehman, p. 11 Corbis/M. Gerber, p. 12 Corbis/R. Jack, p. 14 Corbis/J. Choo, p. 21 Corbis/C. Lovell, p. 30 Corbis Sygma/J. Jedell, p. 37 Corbis/L. Bobbé, p. 38 Corbis/M. St. Maur Shiel (old hotel), p. 44 Corbis/ R. Roa (Sean Connery), Corbis/E. Robert (Harrison Ford), Corbis/R. F. Folkks (Kylie Minogue), Corbis/R. Hellestad (Pavarotti), Corbis/M. Gerber (Julia Roberts), Corbis/M. MacLeod (J. K. Rowling), p. 45 Corbis/J. Luis Pelaez, Inc., p. 52 R. Horrox; p. 48 Getty Images/Time Life Pictures/John Maier Jr; p. 16 The Moviestore Collection/Arts Council of England/BBC/Studio Canal/Tiger Aspect Productions/WT2/Working Title Films (Billy Elliott); p. 36 Rex Features.

Every effort has been made to reach the copyright holders; the publishers would be pleased to hear from anyone whose rights they have unknowingly infringed.